D0646794

Thinking Green!

Thinking Green!

Essays on Environmentalism, Feminism, and Nonviolence

PETRA K. KELLY

Foreword by Peter Matthiessen

PARALLAX
PRESS

Parallax Press
Berkeley, California

Parallax Press
P.O. Box 7355
Berkeley, California 94707

Design by Ayelet Maida/Legacy Media, Inc. Cover photograph of
Petra Kelly, 1983, by Ellerbrock Schafft, Bilderberg. "The Legacy
of Petra K. Kelly," by Mark Hertsgaard, was originally published
in *Vanity Fair,* January 1993; reprinted with permission of the
author.

Special thanks to the Ira-Hiti Foundation for the generous grant
that allowed us to complete the work on this book.

Library of Congress Cataloging-in-Publication Data

Kelly, Petra Karin, 1947-1992
    Thinking green! : essays on environmentalism, feminism,
and nonviolence / Petra K. Kelly.
     p. cm.
   ISBN 0-938077-62-7 : $18.00
   1. Greenmovement. 2. Environmentalism.
  3. Feminism. 4. Nonviolence. I. Title.
   JA75.8.K464   1994
   324.243'08—dc20   94-8989
                                    CIP

Contents

Preface

Some months after Parallax Press' 1991 publication of Petra Kelly's *The Anguish of Tibet*, we reached an agreement with Ms. Kelly to publish a book of her writings about ecology, feminism, nonviolence, human rights, North-South relations, and a host of related topics. She forwarded to us more than one thousand pages of speeches, interviews, and articles, which editor Andrew Cooper began organizing into this book.

In September 1992, when Petra Kelly, Gert Bastian, Stephen Batchelor, and I met over dinner in Berlin to discuss the book's development, Petra gave me another thousand pages of documents. We talked at length about Tibet, the rise of neo-Nazism in Germany, and many other topics, and shared our mutual excitement about the book's progress and the work needed to complete it. She also asked in great detail about my wife's brother, who had just been in an auto accident. Petra was always extremely thoughtful and concerned, not only about the big issues, but about everyday people and events. She and Gert gave us a box of Berlin chocolates, and also a piece of the Berlin Wall, which she herself was so instrumental in bringing down.

In less than a month, Petra and Gert were found dead, having been shot in their small house outside of Bonn.

Although there has never been an extensive investigation, official or unofficial, the authorities concluded that Gert shot Petra, then himself. I continue to find that difficult to believe or accept, as they both had been so energetic and forward-looking such a short time before.

After a period of mourning and reflection, we at Parallax Press decided to go ahead and complete this project, with the help of many of Petra's close friends and colleagues around the world, including Charlene Spretnak, Sara Parkin, Claire Greensfelder, Cora Weiss, Peter Matthiessen, Eleanor LeCain, Abdul Aziz Said, Philip Bogdonoff, Kirkpatrick Sale, Vandana Shiva, Tom Ginsburg, Maria Duerr, and Mark Hertsgaard. Special thanks are due to Andy Cooper, who combed through all of Petra's papers, established the outline of the book, and did all of the initial editing, and Margaret Kelly, Petra's mother, whose cooperation and support have been most heartening.

Our deepest wish for this book is that it serve as a tribute to Petra K. Kelly, one of the great peacemakers of the twentieth century, and that it also serve in some small way to help bring about the kind of world Petra worked so hard all her life to create.

Arnold Kotler, Publisher
Parallax Press
Berkeley, California
March 1994

Foreword

PETER MATTHIESSEN

Petra Karin Kelly worked with tireless dedication for the most vital causes of our times—peace, human rights, the environment—with an intense morality and selflessness that fairly shone in a public world of expedience, compromise, and greed. Indeed, her pioneer work as a founding spirit of the German Green Party remains an inspiration to organizations and individuals around the world. *Thinking Green!*, an edited collection of her talks, is an impassioned, clear, and cogent exposition of the critical ideas in a burning crusade for humanity that became her life and brought about her death.

The failure of traditional military philosophy, with its hollow phrases like "just war" and "surgical strikes," was made tragically apparent by the Gulf War. The mass murder of innocent people did not solve any problems, but only created a host of new ones.... The macabre scenario of Desert Storm proved many of the warnings and predictions we Greens have been expressing for so many years. In the almost prophetic peace manifesto published just after the Green Party was founded, we highlighted the devastating consequences of a consumer lifestyle and manufacturing methods that are based on the steady flow of natural resources recklessly squandered, leading to the violent appropriation of foreign raw materials. In this light, the Gulf War was a harbinger of future conflicts that will arise in the global struggle for increasingly scarce natural resources. (*Thinking Green!* pages 121-122)

There can be only one answer concerning when to start Green politics at every electoral level in the United States: right now. *Because of the need for a low-energy future; because the Earth's remaining rainforests are being destroyed to meet the interest on debt repayments from poor to rich countries; because over 20 million Americans do not have enough to eat; because we must divert funds from military spending in order to solve terminal environmental, economic, and social problems; because human rights and civil liberties cannot be matters of political expediency; because we must replace consumption with conservation as society's driving force; because we can no longer ignore or neglect the years of warning signals telling us that we have come face to face with the natural limits of what we can take from the Earth; because the Earth has no emergency exit; because we can no longer sit by and watch Western governments be driven by endless expansion of consumption and by the futile goal of economic growth at any cost—for these and countless other desperate reasons, we must present Green alternatives in the U.S.A.* (*Thinking Green!* page 131)

Together with her companion Gert Bastian—a German general who left the Army after protesting the deployment of American missiles in Europe, and worked unceasingly thereafter for pacifist causes—Petra Kelly persevered bravely against political apathy and cynicism, calling for an end to the nuclear menace, the shocking violations of human rights occurring in Tibet, and the resurgence of neo-Nazi gangs in her own country, which, according to press reports, have been sending threatening letters to Greens leaders.

I first met Petra Kelly and Gert Bastian at an environmental conference at Morelia, in Mexico, in late August and early September of 1991, a conference based not only on "the Environment" but on many of the problems that are part of it—human rights, the survival of indigenous peoples, nuclear disaster and pollution, the future of the planet. Many of the conference participants were scientists, and most had special interest in one or two related fields; for Kelly and Bastian, all problems were of special interest, even those they had not encountered before, and this interest was not abstract, intellectual, but expressed itself at once in deep concern for the human beings affected.

For example, the nuclear physicist Vladimir Chernousenko, as a consequence of his work at the Chernobyl "cleanup," was chronically ill throughout the conference, and Petra and Gert were among the first to visit him in the hospital and solicit financial help among the rest of us, and they persisted in this faithfully once the conference was over, organizing support for him in Europe until the day they died.

A few months after Morelia, I was giving a talk in Miami when I spotted Gert and Petra waving and smiling, right in the first row. She was in Miami for a feminist convention, and had discovered—very little escaped her attention—that I was in town, too. We had supper that evening after the talk, and again the next evening—there were always so many ideas to exchange with Petra, talking and laughing with that glee in life, at the same time weeping with frustration and real pain over the many things that hurt her, both emotions twinkling in those dark eyes at the same time, like sun in rain.

In a group, Petra bubbled over with her plans and often did most of the talking, but with just the three of us, she was much calmer, and content to let Major General Bastian, former commander of the 12th Tank Division, talk about their common projects. Though he deferred to her (as to a hurricane), this kindly man was passionate in his quiet way, speaking at moments with cold irony and true contempt for the cowardice and hypocrisy so epidemic among so-called world leaders who were not true leaders, merely politicians, not only willing but eager to risk the future of humanity with any compromise at all that might grease the skids for their own reelection.

One exception, of course, was His Holiness the Dalai Lama, of whom Petra always spoke with the greatest respect and affection, and we also discussed other such heroes as Gandhi and Cesar Chavez, whose outrage at social injustice drove them to ignore contemptible excuses such as *What can just one little person do?* As Petra and Gert knew better than most, that attitude in their own land had done much to let loose the Nazi evil, and might do it again, in any land, if we were not vigilant. (Lately I have been quoted as commenting that, due to certain restraints on the police, the U.S., compared to many other countries, "is a very easy country to be brave in"—*if you are the right color,* I meant to add. As Kelly points out, "The U.S. Constitution isn't bad. It offers a lot of scope for resistance. But it's not enough to say, 'We've got a good democracy.' We must develop and improve it."

We agreed, passionately, that all of the critical problems we were discussing were related (*"Questions of international law and human rights are indivisible"*—*Thinking Green!* page 79) and that every one of them might be solved if *everyone* did *something*—nothing showy or heroic, necessarily, just something for the common welfare, if only a strong letter to a politician or the local newspaper. Not that the talk was grim—the talk was fun! Petra had a great infectious laugh like a little girl, and Gert, too, had a dry laconic humor. He seemed tired, but living with Petra was tiring, and both admitted it.

In June 1992, Petra rang up to ask that I telephone Gert in a German hospital, to help cheer him up after a crippling accident he had suffered in April. He sounded fine, of course, since he was ever gallant. I was in Asia for most of that summer and did not speak with them again until September, before they left for the World Uranium Hearing in Salzburg. This time it was Gert who called from Bonn, sounding well and happy and enthusiastic, to ask me to endorse Petra's nomination for the Andrei Sakharov Award; next came a letter from Petra with the usual exclamation marks all over everything, to ask if I would write the foreword for this book. In *Thinking Green!* this astonishing woman meant to deal with the Environment, Nonviolence, Nuclear Proliferation, Feminist Principles, Problems in Eastern Europe, the Suppression of Tibet— in short, the lot!

How shocking, then, that on October 19, a Monday evening, their executed bodies were found in their house in Bonn, having lain undiscovered for at least two weeks, possibly three. On Tuesday, well before an autopsy or post-mortem could be performed, the police announced, "We are certain of one thing, which is that a third person was not responsible for the deaths...." Perhaps they were right, but *how* were they so certain? And why did they feel obliged to make such a premature declaration, knowing that any secret service (or well-trained operatives) could fake every circumstance that was described, and in the light of the many well-known threats that Gert and Petra had received—these same police who had certified Petra Kelly as "an endangered person"!

I did not know Gert and Petra long—nor even, in the usual sense, "well"—and I am aware (they were quite undefended about it) that they had serious financial and emotional problems. Even so, they did *not* sound like people who would die within two weeks in a murder-suicide, far less in a suicide pact, less still in a willful act without a note of explanation to close friends or even the aged relatives they were close to and taking care of. (Yet there *were* letters, written by Gert that very evening, an innocuous letter to his wife, an innocuous business letter to his attorney, which was not only unfinished but broken off in the middle of a word. That letter was still in his typewriter, which was still running when the bodies were discovered two weeks later, but there was no word of any kind to the thousands of people for whom they embodied the courage and commitment and hope that might still spare our world from the fate we seem so determined to visit upon ourselves.)

This is one reason all their friends are so disturbed—this very strong scent of unfinished business. I ranged around the house and tossed in bed, unable to make my peace with such news for days after—something was wrong, something was missing, something was not known.

Or perhaps the "something that was missing" was simply Gert and Petra—"these pure, blameless, and holy children of our universe," as Vladimir Chernousenko called these extraordinary people who gave themselves to us so bravely and so selflessly.

I think how sad their friend the Dalai Lama must be, all the more so as a Buddhist who believes that the manner and the moment of dying is so critical to well-being in a future life. How wonderful that such a meditative man would encourage Petra in her activism, saying, "I will do your meditation for you."

I had told them in Morelia how shocked American Indian people were that white people seemed so willing to leave such a polluted and diminished world for our children and grandchildren, and Petra had grown increasingly interested in the symbolic case of Leonard Peltier and other Indian problems. In what may have been her final article (it appeared in *Newsday*, October 22, 1992, three days after the discovery of her body and several weeks after her death), she wrote about her hopes for a shift in U.S. policy after the election, beginning a long list of the critical problems that needed to be "healed" (not solved, notice, but *healed*—that was her way) with "initiating a policy of justice for native Americans."

I reread her letters. A wild letter in March 1992 concluded:

We wish you were here. We feel very close to you.... Hope you won't forget us!

I won't forget them. Nobody who knew them will forget these vital, generous people. They are gone too soon, leaving a great hole in our hearts and in our lives.

Peter Matthiessen
Sagaponack, New York
January 1993

Thinking Green!

Introduction

*"I still believe that people
are good at heart."* —Anne Frank [1]

My sister, Grace Patricia, died of eye cancer in 1970, at the age of ten. I always wonder why such a beautiful girl had to die so young. Was it because of the nuclear power plants that kept breaking down near our home in Virginia, or because her father, my stepfather, was in Hiroshima as a young soldier just a few weeks after the atomic bomb exploded? Was the cancer worsened by the radiation treatment she received? When Grace died, I resolved to do everything in my power to inform people about the military and civilian uses of nuclear technology and to participate in whatever ways I could to campaign nonviolently against it. I vowed to dedicate my life to finding out why so many millions have become cancer patients and why we are all atomic hostages in this radioactive age. There has always been a mysterious connection between Grace and me. I know she is watching me and guiding me in my work. The way she lived—smiling, loving, hoping, and enduring so much pain—has given me all the guidance and inspiration I have needed to carry on my political, ecological, and feminist work.

I was born and raised in Germany, but because I lived in the United States for ten years, I have both a German

---

[1] *The Diary of Anne Frank* (New York: Bantam Books, 1952), p. 263.

and an American perspective. I am from Günzberg, the Bavarian town on the Danube that is also the hometown of Dr. Joseph Mengele, the "Angel of Death" of Auschwitz. Until I was thirteen, I was raised by my grandmother, an antifascist before and during the time of Hitler. Omi (a German term of endearment for "grandmother") was always extremely courageous. As a war widow, even through the hardest times, she managed to take care of my mother and me. When I was six, she began to read to me from newspapers and newsmagazines, explaining each article in a simple yet precise way. It was clear to her that women must be allowed to pursue whatever interests they choose. Except for my years in the United States, Omi has always been at my side. During the 1970s and '80s, she walked with me in the streets of Germany and Ireland, protesting nuclear power plants and weapons, police terror, and the criminalization of pacifists, actively supporting me through four electoral campaigns, helping with all the grassroots work even in the harshest weather. Whenever I feel I cannot go on, I think of her and I feel a resurgence of strength. The way she has lived her life—with honesty, modesty, and courage—has had a profound influence on me.

My mother has also been a very important influence. She needed no men to help her determine her life and her future. After an unhappy marriage and divorce in Günzberg, she set an example of integrity and independence. She too got much of her energy from Omi.

I was a devout Catholic. I attended convent school and, as a young girl, contemplated becoming a nun so I could play guitar and sing to the children in Africa, while, at the same time, trying to feed them and help them be healthy again. But I broke with the Catholic church when I realized I could no longer be part of a patriarchal club of men dressed in black who determine how women all over the world should be subordinated. I am deeply religious and feel whole and equal to men, and I do not need an authoritarian, male institution to help me find my own inner truth. I have searched for gods and goddesses of cosmic energy, light, and love, and have found much wisdom in Eastern religions. Through contact and communication with my Tibetan foster child, Nima, who lives in Northern India, I have become acquainted with Tantric and Buddhist beliefs. To me, all forms of religion seem to have at their heart the one truth that unites us, which is love.

After my mother remarried, we moved to the U.S., landing first in Georgia, then Virginia, and finally Washington, D.C., where I attended the American University's School of International Service. Two professors there, Abdul Aziz Said and Albert Mott, helped me become a critical thinker and very antiauthoritarian. Dr. Said conveyed to me the essence of international politics as active solidarity with the poor, the oppressed, and the exploited. He infused his teaching of international relations with a deep element of spirituality. Dr. Mott, one of the most challenging history professors one could hope to meet, forced me to confront my German past as no one before had. Studying with him, I was able to attain a new perspective on my roots.

Elie Wiesel reminds us constantly that what happened once can happen again for the same reasons and very likely with the same victims. That is why the Holocaust must never be forgotten or forgiven. In my convent school in Bavaria, I learned nothing whatsoever about the Holocaust, about the crimes committed by the German people.

It was only after coming to the United States that I was confronted by my teachers with Anne Frank, Auschwitz, Bergen-Belsen, Treblinka, Buchenwald, Ravensbrück, Dachau, Fascist crimes, and the "silent consent" of the German people. In the U.S. I was asked what happened to the Nazi leaders, and it disturbed me to discover that most of them had not been punished or were released earlier than expected. In fact, key persons involved with Nazi industry, jurisdiction, and security were treated with astonishing generosity.

After ten years in the U.S. (1960 to 1970), I returned to Europe and soon became an administrator in the European Economic Community, assigned to social, environmental, health, and education issues. In European politics, I worked within the West German Social Democratic Party (SPD) as a loyal supporter of Willy Brandt until the mid-1970s, when a few friends and I began to think about leaving the Social Democrats to create a new party based on ecological, feminist, and anti-militaristic principles. Many friends at the time felt that this would be a negative act, that it would be better to work within the existing SPD to move it towards Green concerns. But as the old pathways became more twisted and tangled, I was determined to dedicate all my energy toward the creation of a new "anti-party" party.

In 1979, we founded the Green Party *(Die Grünen)* in West Germany. We received 3.2 percent, about a million votes, in our first foray into national politics, and I knew we were on track. In 1982, we won 5.6 percent, and I was one of 27 Green Party members awarded a seat in Parliament. During my Parliamentary tenure, I was on the very male Foreign Relations Committee, and also in the Western European Union Parliamentary Assembly, and the

Sub-Committee on European Affairs and Disarmament. I worked on issues of human rights, foreign policy, neutrality, disarmament, children's cancer, and many ecological concerns.

After nearly eight years of effective work in Parliament, shifting the national debate to include many Green issues and introducing a new kind of grassroots democracy, we Greens failed to receive the necessary 5 percent of the national vote in the December 1990 elections. Many critics now say that our vision of an "anti-party" party failed, but I believe that it was not our vision that failed but the way we practiced our political lifestyle—always arguing and bickering among our various factions.

But, "I still believe that people are good at heart." These words of Anne Frank motivate me to go on searching for nonviolent methods to wake people up and transform our nuclear age into an age of peace, justice, feminism, and environmental awareness. To think Green is nothing less than to heal the human spirit and completely reallocate our resources and priorities. We need nothing less if we are to survive and flourish in the twenty-first century.

Chapter One

Women and Power

*"True emancipation begins neither at
the polls nor in the courts. It begins
in women's soul."* —Emma Goldman [1]

As a teenager growing up into a young woman, I was enraged when I saw how women have been obliterated from the pages of history and the pages of the Bible. Women were subordinated and dependent on men for their realization and value, always needing men as their path to fulfillment. I began to read Rosa Luxemburg's writings, particularly her prison diaries, and to search through biographies of Alexandra Kollontai, George Sand, Emma Goldman, Helen Keller, and other women who have put their very special stamp on history but have been mostly ignored by male historians and male scholars. I set out to rediscover these brave women. I never had much respect for Marx, Engels, and all the other dogmatic macho men who theorized and philosophized about the working classes and capital while, at the same time, discriminating against their wives and children and leading the lives of "academic *pashas*," always being rejuvenated by their wives and mistresses. They couldn't even cook or clean or sew or take care of themselves. They always needed women for their most basic needs.

---

[1] Emma Goldman, "The Tragedy of Woman's Emancipation," in *The Traffic in Women and Other Essays on Feminism* (Albion, California: Times Change Press, 1970), p. 14.

Men's domination of women is deep and systemic, and it is accepted around the world by most men and many women as "natural," as something that somehow cannot be changed. But norms of human behavior do change. Because the oppression of women is so deeply embedded in our societies and our psyches, it continues to be invisible, even to those who are working to overcome other forms of injustice. Feminism is considered by many people to be one aspect of social justice, but to me it is a principle in and of itself. To rid the world of nuclear weapons and poverty, we must end racism and sexism. As long as white males hold all of the social and economic power, women and people of color will continue to be discriminated against, and poverty and the military mentality will continue unabated. We cannot just analyze structures of domination and oppression. We must also practice disobedience in our own lives, starting by disobeying all systems of male domination.

The system in which men have more value and more social and economic power than women is found throughout the world—East and West, North and South. Women suffer both from structural oppression and from individual men. Too many movements for social justice accept the assumptions of male dominance and ignore the oppression of women, but patriarchy pervades both our political and our personal lives. Feminism rejects all forms of male dominance and affirms the value of women's lives and experiences. It recognizes that no pattern of domination is necessary and seeks to liberate women and men from the structures of dominance that characterize patriarchy.

Many women are beginning to reject the existing systems and styles of male politics. Whether at Greenham Common, Comiso, Australia, Belau, protecting the Himalayan forests, or working for peace in Eastern Europe, women have been stirred to action. Motivated to act on our own, not only as mothers and nurturers but also as leaders in a changing world, we must stand up as women and become elected to political and economic offices throughout the world, so we can change the policies and structures from those of death to those of life. We do not need to abrogate our positive, feminist principles of loving, caring, showing emotions, and nurturing. Every individual has both feminine and masculine qualities. We should not relieve men of their responsibility to transform themselves, to develop caring human qualities and become responsible for childcare, housework, and all other essential support work. We will never be able to reclaim the Earth if men do not give up their privileges and share these basic tasks with women. Children are not just the responsibility of their mothers.

The scientific revolution of the seventeenth century contained in it the seeds of today's oppressive technologies. If we trace the myths and metaphors associated with the conquest of nature, we will realize how much we are under the sway of masculine institutions and ideologies. Masculine technology and patriarchal values have prevailed in Auschwitz, Dresden, Hiroshima, Nagasaki, Vietnam, Iran, Iraq, Afghanistan, and many other parts of the world. The ultimate result of unchecked, terminal patriarchy will be ecological catastrophe or nuclear holocaust.

Feminism is about alleviating women's powerlessness. Women must share half the Earth and half the Sky, on our own terms and with our own self-determined values. Feminism seeks to redefine our very modes of existence and to transform nonviolently the structures of male dominance. I am not saying that women are inherently better than men. Overturning patriarchy does not mean replacing men's dominance with women's dominance. That would merely maintain the patriarchal pattern of dominance. We need to transform the pattern itself. The work of feminist women and profeminist men is to liberate everyone from a system that is oppressive to women and restrictive to men, and to restore balance and harmony between women and men and between masculine and feminine values in society and within each of us. Feminists working in the peace and ecology movements are sometimes viewed as kind, nurturing Earth mothers, but that is too comfortable a stereotype. We are not meek and we are not weak. We are angry—on our own behalf, for our sisters and children who suffer, and for the entire planet—and we are determined to protect life on Earth.

Green women work together with men on issues like ecology and disarmament. But we must also assert women's oppression as a central concern, for our experience is that men do not take women's oppression as seriously as other causes. There is a clear and profound relationship between militarism, environmental degradation, and sexism. Any commitment to social justice and nonviolence that does not address the structures of male domination of women is incomplete. We will work with our Green brothers, but we will not be subservient to them. They must demonstrate their willingness to give up the privileges of membership in the male caste.

There is a saying: Where power is, women are not. Women must be willing to be powerful. Because we bear scars from the ways men have used their power over us, women often want no part of power. To a certain extent, this is good sense. Patriarchal power has brought us acid rain, global warming, military states, and countless cases of private suffering. We have all seen men whose power has caused them to lose all sense of reality, decency, and imagination, and we are right to fear such power. But playing an active part in society, on an equal footing with men, does not mean adopting the old thought patterns and strategies of the patriarchal world. It means putting our own ideas of an emancipatory society into practice. Rather than emulating Margaret Thatcher and others who loyally adapt themselves to male values of hierarchy, we must find our own definitions of power that reflect women's values and women's experience. Jean Baker Miller points out how women, though closed out of male dominions of power, experience great power in the daily work of nurturing others.[2] This is not power *over* others, but power *with* others, the kind of shared power that has to replace patriarchal power.

Women in the Green movement are committed to fighting the big wars—the destruction of nature, imperial politics, militarism, and the like. But we are just as determined to end the little wars that take place against women every day, often invisibly. Women's suffering seems so normal and is so pervasive that it is scarcely noticed. These restrictions, degradations, and acts of violence are so embedded in our societies that they appear natural, but they are not natural. The system of which these are a part has been constructed over centuries by laws and through institutions that were developed by men and excluded women. We want to end these forms of oppression by doing away with the power and mentality that produced and maintains them.

---

[2] Jean Baker Miller, *Toward a New Psychology of Women* (Boston: Beacon Press, 1986. Second edition).

There are many structures of domination—nation over nation, class over class, race over race, humans over nature. But domination of women by men is a constant feature within every other aspect of oppression. Male dominance is typical of other patterns of domination across all cultural divides. It is the basis of the systems of politics that have brought the world to its present, extreme state. It is the pattern that connects acts of individual rape with the ecological rape of our planet.

In *Sisterhood Is Global*, Robin Morgan describes the daily war against women:

> While women represent half the global population and one-third of the labor force, they receive only one-tenth of the world income and own less than one percent of world property. They also are responsible for two-thirds of all working hours.... Not only are females most of the poor, the starving, and the illiterate, but women and children constitute more than 90 percent of all refugee populations. Women outlive men in most cultures and therefore *are* the elderly of the world, as well as being the primary caretakers of the elderly.... In industrialized countries, women still are paid only one-half to three-quarters of what men earn at the same jobs, still are ghettoized into lower-paying, "female-intensive" job categories, and still are the last hired and the first fired.[3]

Just as patriarchy is global, so too is sisterhood. The most pernicious of all patriarchal tactics is to keep women divided. We feminists in Europe and North America have

---

[3] Robin Morgan, "Planetary Feminism: The Politics of the 21st Century," in *Sisterhood Is Global* (Garden City: Doubleday, 1984), pp. 1-2.

been so occupied with our own struggles that we have neglected our solidarity with women's struggles in other parts of the world. Today, and perhaps throughout history, indigenous women's movements have mobilized to defend human life and nature. Women of the Chipko movement are defending the forests in India. In Belau, women are demanding nuclear-free constitutions. Women have been instrumental in the democratic movements in the Philippines, South Africa, Central America, and among indigenous peoples everywhere. In the Middle East, Israeli and Palestinian feminists have maintained a dialogue toward peace based on the recognition of their common experience as women. It is essential that we work with and learn from our sisters throughout the world. Feminist women and profeminist men must recognize the particular urgency of women's struggles in the Third World. Over the last thirty-five years, the gap between rich and poor nations has widened. As the poor become poorer, women, being the poorest of the poor, suffer the most acutely. When one considers women as a single worldwide caste, it is not difficult to see that, despite some progress, our situation remains dire.

Third World women are oppressed both by national and international injustices and by family systems that give husbands, fathers, and brothers absolute priority. Even where economic development benefits poor families, it is often of no benefit to poor women, for inequality and exploitation exist within families as well as between them. The unfair sexual distribution of power, resources, and responsibilities is legitimized by ancient traditions, socialized into women's own attitudes, enshrined in law, and enforced when necessary by male violence.

Women constitute the largest group of landless laborers in the world. Though they do much of the work in most agricultural regions, because land ownership is generally the domain of men, women have even less security than male tenants or employees. In many places, a woman may be evicted by her husband upon divorce or by her husband's male relatives upon his death. Membership in cooperatives is often restricted to men. While cash crop programs boost men's incomes, women are called upon to help with the extra work, while their own food crops are shifted to more distant or less fertile plots. Agricultural extension services are staffed almost exclusively by men and addressed to helping men.

Industrial development and urbanization have worsened an already unjust division of labor between women and men. Factory production wipes out domestic handicrafts businesses on which women depend, but women are at a disadvantage competing with men for factory jobs because their educational qualifications are lower and they are more likely to be raising children. Two-thirds of the world's illiterate are women. In Nairobi, half the working women earn less than a poverty wage, compared to 20 percent of the men. Studies in both developed and developing countries reveal that men enjoy more free time than women. A survey in Zaire assessed that men did only 30 percent of the amount of work women do. In most of Africa and Asia, women work, on average, sixteen-hour days, jeopardizing their own health and that of their children.

Besides housework and childcare, many heavy chores are universally relegated to women. For Masai women of Kenya's Rift Valley, fetching up to fifty pounds of water at a time can take up to five hours a day. Gathering a similar weight of wood for cooking may be a two-hour job, and much longer in areas of extensive deforestation. The notorious "double day," in which women work as a full unit of economic production and also do all the unpaid house-work and childcare, is spreading in agrarian societies as well as in industrial ones. It is one of the longest lasting of women's oppressions. Throughout the Third World, women are dispossessed, overlooked, and overworked. The examples given here barely scratch the surface. We who live in industrialized countries must challenge the sexism of our own countries' programs of international development aid. Legal discriminations must be removed, and women must have equal access to the benefits of these programs. To those who say it is not up to us in the industrialized world to tell those in the Third World how to live, I agree. Let it be up to those societies to determine their own courses. But let *everyone* be included, not only the men.

Courageous women in the ecology, human rights, and feminist movements in the Third World have taught me about the link between the violation of nature and the violation and marginalization of women. Meeting aboriginal women in Australia, women in the alternative movements in India, and feminist ecologists around the globe, I have seen how ecofeminists in the Third World are deeply challenging many concepts the West has defended until now. Indian physicist Vandana Shiva describes how Western science ignores or excludes certain bodies of knowledge while elevating itself. This arrogance, she tells us, constitutes a great threat to our planet.

> While Third World women have privileged access to survival expertise, their knowledge is inclusive, not exclusive. The ecological categories with which they think and act can become the categories of liberation for all, for men as well as for women, for

West as well as the non-West, and for the human as
well as the non-human elements of the earth.[4]

Many Greens, including myself, have been inspired
by the work of nonviolent men like Mahatma Gandhi,
Martin Luther King, Jr., and Cesar Chavez. We know far
less about contributions to nonviolence by women like
Dorothy Day, Rosa Parks, and the women in the recent
nonviolent revolutions in Eastern Europe. Invisibility of
women is a familiar pattern of male dominance, even
within otherwise progressive movements. Much of the effectiveness of nonviolent resistance in awakening people's
consciences derives from the willingness of those practicing it to accept suffering. But because women's suffering
is taken for granted, in the eyes of the media and the general public the work of nonviolent women is less note-
worthy and carries less virtue than that of men. Media
coverage of the women at Greenham Common, for example, who endured great hardship camping out during one
of England's harshest winters to protest American militarism, concentrated not on what they were doing or why,
but on their families who were "left behind to cope" without them.

Women's power arouses great hostility in the male-
dominated media. As a woman active and visible in politics, I experience this often. In the early 1980s, when I was
a speaker for the Green Party in Parliament, a reporter
asked in an interview what was wrong with me, an intelligent, clever, attractive, and unmarried young woman, that
would cause me to be involved in politics, a realm he
clearly considered the exclusive province of men. (Perhaps he thought I was looking for a husband.) I turned

[4] Vandana Shiva, *Staying Alive: Women, Ecology and Development* (London:
Zed Books, 1989), p. 244.

and walked out. The women present—the staff, the studio's cleaning women—supported me, but the reporter, to this day, has never understood why I left the interview. In 1985, *Penthouse* published a degrading pornographic cartoon of me; I brought suit against them.

Incidents like these should not surprise anyone. The media, for the most part, perpetuate double standards and sexist stereotypes: Women are sex toys for men; women's lives count less than those of men; women who assert their independence and power are in some way defective. Freedom of the press is one of the most important freedoms, and it must never be curtailed. But protection from sexism must also be recognized as a full human right. I do not believe that freedom of the press includes the right to sell sexist images of women to the general public.

As women assert ourselves, we face the question of whether we should seek access to every male arena of power, even at the price of giving up feminist principles. My own feeling is that we cannot forsake women's liberation by accepting a patriarchal interpretation of equality. We must work from our own values and elevate their influence to those of men. It cannot be part of feminist logic to seek access to all professions, no matter how inhumane. In Germany this question has been focused on the issue of women's conscription into the military. Under the cloak of equality, men in the federal government have moved to pass legislation calling for conscription of women. It is ridiculous that the equality we want is possible in the military but not in other sectors of society. I do not want to see women stand equal with our brothers, fathers, and husbands in nuclear command centers, on battle fronts, or in meeting rooms where the deaths of thousands are planned. As one woman working for peace said, "To establish more equal relations between the sexes, rather than training women to kill, let men learn to nurture life." For centuries, we have been locked out of power in male-dominated societies. We should not now allow ourselves to be cynically manipulated by men who wish to exploit our legitimate needs and aspirations by granting us power on their terms to serve their ends. We must work for ends consistent with feminist values. There should not be women in the military. Take the men out.

Because the world's governments are unable to sustain and guarantee peace, the women at Greenham Common formed a living chain around a military weapons base. I call upon women everywhere, young and old, to form a chain around the world, to resist those who say war is inevitable, and to love only those men who are willing to speak out against the violence. We all need to join together—women uncorrupted by male power and men opposed to violence who wish to break out of the rigid patriarchal institutions.

Throughout history, male-led social movements have always been mere exchanges of power, while the basic structure of dominant hierarchies has remained. The liberation of women and men from the bonds of patriarchy is essential to the work of building a peaceful, just, and ecological society. I often hear people arguing about the world's many evils and which should be the first confronted. This fragmentary approach is itself part of the problem, reflecting the linear, hierarchical nature of patriarchal thinking that fails to grasp the complexity of living systems. What is needed is a perspective that integrates the many problems we face and approaches them holistically. Working towards such a future begins by living now in accord with what we seek to bring forth.

Chapter Two

Creating an Ecological Economy

"Is this not a precious home for us Earthlings? Is this not worth our love? Does it not deserve all the inventiveness and courage and generosity of which we are capable to preserve it from degradation and destruction and, by doing so, to secure our own survival?" —Barbara Ward and Rene Dubos [1]

Ecologist Aldo Leopold had an experience in which he began "thinking like a mountain." He came to see humans as "plain citizens" of the natural world, writing, "We abuse land because we regard it as a commodity belonging to us. When we see land as a community to which we belong, we may begin to use it with love and respect."[2]

Like the mind-set that places men above women, whites above blacks, and rich above poor, the mentality that places humans above nature is a dysfunctional delusion. It is based on the principle of domination. We humans take our Earth for granted and never hesitate to exploit it and its other inhabitants to gratify our immediate wants. We have to understand that we are part of nature, not outside of it. What we do to the Earth, we do to ourselves. Understanding our interconnectedness with all life is the essence of ecological politics and an ecological economy.

We need very little of what consumer society tells us. Lavish consumption brings only a crude sort of gratification. Cultivating the intuitions of our identity with the whole of life in all its diversity brings delight to the heart

---

[1] Barbara Ward and Rene Dubos, *Only One Earth: The Care and Maintenance of a Small Planet* (New York: Norton, 1972), p. 220.

[2] Quoted in Bill Devall and George Sessions, *Deep Ecology* (Salt Lake City: G.M. Smith, 1985), p.68.

and a deeper and more durable fulfillment. These intuitions are essential for a life based on values, and they are also the basis for political action. The personal transformation to what Arne Naess calls "a life simple in means but rich in ends" is itself a political act.[3] If we want to transform society in an ecological way, we must profoundly transform ourselves.

E. F. Schumacher said that a nonviolent and gentle attitude toward nature must be the basis for all politics:

> The violent and aggressive approach to the natural world is fed by human greed for short-term material gain without care of the long-term ill effects on other generations. Anyone analyzing Western economics will realize very soon how violent and aggressive the Western approach has been up to now in this area. Western economic thinking depends upon insatiable consumption—demanding more and more and larger and larger goods and services to be available at all times. But where is the basic ethic of restraint?

In telling us that "small is beautiful," Schumacher points to a consciousness of the limits in which we must live in order not to degrade our environment and ourselves.[4]

In fact, we have already far exceeded those limits, and we continue to do so. Yet no official economic policy has taken seriously the accelerating biological holocaust devastating the Earth. All of the established parties refuse to

---

[3] Arne Naess, *Ecology, Community and Lifestyle: Outline of an Ecosophy* (New York: Cambridge University Press, 1989).

[4] E.F. Schumacher, *Small Is Beautiful* (New York: Harper & Row, 1973).

recognize the need to curtail economic growth and not promote it if we are to avert a complete ecological catastrophe. Despite all of the environmental evidence that their way of doing business is destroying life, governments continue to make decisions based on short-term economic gain. In the end, their economies will pull the rugs out from under their own feet and bring the rest of us down with them. The Earth simply cannot sustain unlimited exploitation.

We in the Greens say that we have borrowed the Earth from our children. Green politics is about having just "enough" and not "more," and this runs counter to all of the economic assumptions of industrial society. We must question those assumptions. The ecological crisis is a crisis of consumption, not of scarcity of resources. The industrialized countries must move from growth-oriented to sustainable economies, with conservation replacing consumption as the driving force. In the Third World, economic and ecological development must be addressed together if we wish to achieve just and sustainable results. But this cannot happen if the North's exploitative policies continue. Ecologically balanced development depends on a just redistribution of wealth from the North to the South. Environmental problems cannot be addressed apart from the economic issues they are linked with. We have to ask, How would an ecological economy function, and what can we do to bring it about?

An ecological economy would measure the prosperity of a society not in terms of the numbers of goods produced, but rather in terms of production methods that conserve the environment, protect human health, and result in durable consumer goods. The measure of value would include clean air, pure water, unpoisoned food, and the flourishing of diverse life forms. In an ecological society, the economy, lifestyles, and consumer expectations would be characterized by considerations of human and environmental health. The economy would not regard industrial growth as its guiding value, but would be guided by respect for life and the inherent worth of nature. The relationship between humans and nature would not be a one-way exploitative process, but a partnership based on interdependence.

The establishment of an ecological economy would require the partial dismantling and conversion of existing industrial systems, in particular those branches of industry that are hazardous to life, above all the nuclear, chemical, and defense industries. Wherever possible and ecologically meaningful, mass industry would be replaced by small, decentralized production units that are sparing in their use of natural resources and produce a minimum of hazardous waste. Decentralized production can be more ecologically sound, more responsive to the needs of workers and the immediate community, and the basis for greater local economic autonomy.

Ecological production would reject the sharp national and international division of labor that has led to large economic imbalances between regions, between city and countryside, and between industrialized nations and the Third World, and that has brought about high transportation costs and correspondingly excessive energy and land requirements. Locating production facilities closer to consumers would reduce transportation costs and energy consumption. These changes are within our means. Their implementation depends only on our will but will require grassroots organizing, because national political leaders cannot see or refuse to recognize the limits of growth, and they lack the vision or the motivation to base their decisions on environmental ethics.

The changes just stated apply only to economies that are already industrialized. What about the developing countries and the traditional and aboriginal societies? Over the years, I have seen many disagreements between the environmental movements in the Western affluent societies whose focus is solely on ecological concerns, and activists in the Third and Fourth Worlds and from oppressed communities within the affluent countries who insist that ecological concerns must be tied to issues of economic justice—the exploitation of the poor by the rich. The rape of the Earth will not be halted simply by the affluent imposing conservation measures on others. The seedbed of ecological destruction is the global division between the rich and the poor. Behind every environmental issue are landless villagers or workers who are forced to destroy nature in order to survive, or governments, banks, or corporations who pursue economic growth without much regard for people or nature. Ben Jackson wrote, "A series of 'Keep Out' signs around the world's forests would not only be morally unacceptable, but with the world's poor still hungry outside, it just would not work." To solve our environmental problems, we must address these economic issues. And conversely, to tackle the grave problems of poverty, we must nurture the environment. To quote Ben Jackson again:

> The environment directly underpins the long-term viability and security of many poor people's livelihoods and culture. Only if soils are cared for, will they keep producing crops or withstand the shocks of natural disasters like drought. The environment is also the medium through which many of their es-

sential needs are met or not met. Health, for example, is often dependent on whether the river or well gives clean drinking water and whether there is decent sanitation.[5]

The transformation of forests into deserts, fertile earth into sunbaked concrete, and running rivers into silted floodwaters show that only through care for the environment can the livelihoods of those most dependent on it be sustained. We cannot allow economic and environmental concerns to be played off against each other. We see this over and over as corporations and governments portray the environmental movement as undermining and disregarding the welfare of humans. It is incumbent upon the environmental movement to find common ground and establish new alliances with groups concerned with peace and social justice, world poverty, and labor issues. These issues are all linked. We can take inspiration from Australia's Green Ban, in which trade unionists refused to work on environmentally damaging projects, even at the cost of jobs and imprisonment.

The lifestyles, policies, and production methods of the industrial countries endanger human existence and can only be maintained through the increasing exploitation of the Third World. An industrial system predicated on the delusion of limitless expansion will, in time, consume its own basis of support. Obviously, such a system cannot be the model for development for the Third World. Ecological development is possible, but we must insist on changing "business as usual."

---

[5] Ben Jackson, *Poverty and the Planet: A Question of Survival* (Harmondsworth: Penguin, 1990).

Poor countries continue to finance rich ones on an enormous scale. Between 1982 and 1987, Third World countries provided a net of more than $220 billion to the wealthy countries, mostly in necessary imports and interest payments for so-called development loans. The debt figure is now more than $1 trillion. In 1989 alone, the World Bank took $724 million more out of the Brazilian economy than it put in. Since taking the World Bank's bitter medicine in 1983, Ghana's debt burden has doubled to an estimated $3 billion. In September 1989, a hearing of the Human Rights Caucus of the U.S. Congress found that more than 1.5 million people are currently being displaced by World Bank projects. Environmentally harmful development projects funded by the World Bank are routinely dropped in the laps of Third World communities without any consultation. While President Bush praised the World Bank and the International Monetary Fund as "paradigms of international cooperation," the truth was stated more accurately in *The New Internationalist:* "The World Bank has turned out to be an ecological Frankenstein, armed with a chain saw."

Profits from the labor of people and the trade in natural resources have, for decades, flowed from South to North. Amazon rainforests are disappearing not because of the needs of the local inhabitants but to supply cheap beef to Northern consumers and charcoal for smelting iron for export. Southeast Asia's forests are being decimated to supply chopsticks for the Japanese and tropical hardwood for Western markets. In order to develop, the Third World countries have to borrow from the North and then pay the interest on these loans by cashing in their natural resources. Many of the mega-projects that have helped establish the debt treadmill are themselves environmentally destructive, such as the proliferation of nuclear power plants. Indebted countries have not just borrowed from their futures, they have mortgaged them. And, as Susan George says, "Nature has put up the collateral."[6] As commodity prices fall and the debt burden spirals, the Third World is trapped in a vicious cycle of having to export more and earn less.

Industrial countries make the world poorer by consuming disproportionate amounts of the world's resources. The U.S., with five percent of the world's population, is responsible for twenty-five percent of its energy consumption. Australia's 16 million people have the same impact on the world's resources as 1.3 billion Africans. The wealthy nations account for 70 percent of worldwide carbon dioxide emissions, 84 percent of chlorofluorocarbon production, and 90 percent of the greenhouse gas emissions, yet they arrogantly call upon the struggling nations to reduce their carbon dioxide emissions while they refuse to do the same. Between 1986 and 1988, over three million tons of wastes were shipped from industrialized to developing countries in exchange for cash payments. This kind of "garbage imperialism" occurs because the poor nations are so desperate for currency that they will sacrifice their own health.

Maneka Gandhi, India's former Minister for the Environment, was pointing in the direction of the truth when she argued that Western governments actively promote environmental catastrophes in the Third World, yet they want to push the entire burden of ecological adjustment on the Third World. The latest trick is to speak of the need for "global solutions," a euphemistic way to shrug off their

---

[6] Susan George, *A Fate Worse Than Debt* (New York: Grove Press, 1988).

role and responsibility in creating these problems. As Vandana Shiva has said, "The North must bear the main burden and end its exploitation of both nature and the South." This grossly unequal distribution of wealth and power threatens everyone. The deepening poverty of two-thirds of humanity and the degradation of the environment are not separate. An "Iron Curtain" still exists separating the North from the South. The Third World debt crisis is just a symptom of a world organized for the benefit of a privileged class that will stop at nothing to maintain its control.

For environmental solutions to be effective, economic imbalances must be redressed. We need sustainable development in the Third World that supports an ecological economic system, a more just distribution of wealth within and among nations, political reforms, and greater access to the knowledge and resources of the North. The South Commission proposed in 1981 a development strategy of self-reliance, recognizing that no country can be developed by outsiders. Development in the Third World must be for the benefit of the people of the Third World. Then the ecological viability of those countries can be maintained. An important step in this process would be the establishment of a "South Bank" as an alternative to the pressures and exploitative practices of the International Monetary Fund and the World Bank.

On the deepest level, the grave damage posed to life on Earth is not a matter of East-West or North-South. The most deadly polarity is between human activities and the life-sustaining capacities of the Earth. As Patricia Mische wrote, "We are at a new point in human history and in the planet's development when it has become critical to reconsider security priorities in light of new threats to life emanating from human assaults on the Earth."[7]

The 1987 International Conference on the Changing Atmosphere concluded that the dangers posed by the greenhouse effect are as great as those of a nuclear war. In greenhouse scenarios, the accumulation of carbon dioxide and other atmospheric gases will trap heat and thereby warm the Earth, causing polar ice caps to melt and the flooding of whole countries. Deserts would expand, resulting in mass starvation and mass migrations. Every ecosystem could potentially be disrupted, with massive extinctions of plant and animal species and the support of human life. If industry and agriculture continue on their present course, these things could happen *within fifty years.*

When compared with such possibilities, notions like national security become meaningless. Wendell Berry writes, "To what point do we defend from foreign enemies a country we are destroying ourselves?"[8] Military policies are among the most destructive, wasteful contributors to environmental degradation. Worldwatch Institute has observed, "Again there is the irony that the pursuit of military might is such a costly endeavor that it drains away the resources urgently needed to protect against the environmental perils that are most likely to jeopardize our security."[9]

Militarization is in direct competition with people's needs for food, health care, and environmental protec-

---

[7] *Breakthrough: Journal of the Prairie Fire Organizing Committee,* Vol. 15 (San Francisco: John Brown Book Club).

[8] Wendell Berry, *Home Economics* (San Francisco: North Point Press, 1987), p. 110.

[9] Michael Renner, "Assessing the Military's War on the Environment," in Lester R. Brown et. al., *State of the World 1991* (New York: W.W. Norton, 1991).

tion. One half of one percent of the world's military expenditure for one year would pay for the farm equipment needed to increase food production and approach agricultural self-sufficiency in the developing world in an ecological way. The Pentagon uses as much petroleum in two and a half weeks as the entire U.S. public transport system uses in a year. There are countless examples of the enormous ecological cost of militarism.

Aboriginal peoples throughout the world have understood for millennia what science has finally come to see: that the Earth and all that is in it are a living, interrelated system. As environmental issues become increasingly urgent and Western models of development become unsustainable, we will need to step out of our Eurocentrism and listen to the wisdom of traditional peoples concerning how to live on the Earth. But, tragically, the very cultures to which we must turn are themselves under attack. Michael Soule observes that the same forces that threaten biological diversity are destroying whole cultures as well, and with them, their legacies of ecological knowledge.

Describing the "frenzy of exploitation" that is ravaging the Earth's green mantle, Soule goes on to say:

> Never in 500 million years of terrestrial evolution has this mantle we call the biosphere been under such a savage attack. Perhaps the hardest thing to grasp is the geological and historical uniqueness of the next few decades. There simply is no precedent for what is happening to the biological fabric of this planet and there are no words to express the horror felt by those who love nature. In our lifetimes, the relentless harrying of habitats, particularly in the tropics, will reduce rainforests, reefs and savannas

to vulnerable and senescent vestiges of their former grandeur and subtlety. Perhaps even more shocking than the unprecedented wave of extinction is the cessation of evolution of new species of large plants and animals—death is one thing, but an end to birth is something else. There is no escaping the conclusion that in our lifetimes, this planet will see a suspension, if not an end, to many ecological and evolutionary processes which have been uninterrupted since the beginnings of paleontological time.[10]

We are facing a wave of extinctions that could exceed in magnitude the wave that destroyed the dinosaurs and many other species 65 million years ago. In the coming decades, thousands and, in time, millions of species will become extinct because of habitat destruction in the tropical forests. These rainforests account for 7 percent of the Earth's land surface, and more than 50 percent of its species. Since 1900, half the world's rainforests have been destroyed, and only 1.5 percent of their original total area is protected. Within one hundred years, that may be all that remains. Fifty acres are destroyed each minute, and an area three times the size of Switzerland disappears each year. Tropical rainforests are among the Earth's most ancient ecosystems, having developed their wealth of genetic diversity under very stable, external conditions over thousands and thousands of years. They constitute a complex, seamless web in which all components are necessary to the whole. Because of this, they are extremely fragile and rarely regenerate. Once they are gone, they will be gone forever.

---

[10] from *The Ten Directions*, Los Angeles, Summer/Fall 1982, p. 8.

Rainforests are called the "lungs of the Earth," because they produce a quarter of the planet's oxygen supply and absorb vast amounts of carbon dioxide. The loss of these habitats could severely disrupt the Earth's climate and hasten the greenhouse effect. Rainforests contain the planet's richest gene pool. Half of all pharmaceuticals include active ingredients found in wild plants. Species whose healing properties we have yet to even discover are being wiped out. Agriculture depends on genetic diversity to develop new crop strains that can withstand constantly evolving disease organisms. The loss of species diversity would compromise our ability to produce the crops we need to heal and feed ourselves. The Greens have demanded that the Third World's debts be exchanged by international agreement for the guaranteed protection of the world's remaining tropical forests. A massive reforestation program, with trees selected for ecological rather than commercial value, must be undertaken. The destructive development programs that threaten the rainforests, including plantation schemes, large dams, ranching schemes, and road programs, must be phased out.

The fact of encroaching ecological catastrophe was tragically brought home to Europeans in the Summer of 1988, when thousands of seals perished in the North Sea and washed ashore along Sweden's coastline. Scientists performing autopsies on the dead seals found traces of *more than a thousand* toxins in the tissue samples. The reasons are not hard to see. The North Sea is a dumping ground for all kinds of industrial waste. Each year, nearly 13,500 tons of lead, 5,600 tons of copper, plus arsenic, cadmium, mercury, and even radioactive wastes flow into the sea from the Rhine, the Meuse, and the Elbe Rivers. The sea is dotted with 4,000 wells and 150 drilling platforms, and pipes connecting these to shore leak 30,000 tons of hydrocarbons each year. Ships dump 145 million tons of ordinary garbage annually. Salmon, sturgeon, oysters, and haddock have simply vanished. Those fish that survive often suffer from skin infections, deformed skeletons, and tumors.

It is important to educate ourselves about the grave assaults on the biosphere—acid rain, desertification, waste accumulation, overpopulation, ozone depletion—to know the grim facts about what we humans are doing to nature. But deeper than statistics and reports, it is essential not to lose sight of our love of creation and desire to preserve it. Common sense tells us that if we continue to damage the environment the results will be horrific. Common decency tells us that the greedy, wasteful destruction of life is wrong.

Siegfried Lenz points out that while we appear to live in peace and comfort, at its foundation is a privileged kind of force that is condoned by public authorities and is making our world more and more uninhabitable. Governments and corporations are taking away lakes and oceans, allowing rivers to die, and turning forests to skeletons. A German court declared that those who resist may be acting on legitimate *moral* grounds but are still *legally* in the wrong. As in many countries, in Germany it is business that makes the rules.

Gary Snyder writes that trees and mountains must be represented in congress and whales must have the right to vote.[11] We in the Greens have tried to further that spirit, to represent those whose voices are not heard in the halls of power—the whales, elephants, dolphins, plants, flow-

---

[11] Gary Snyder, *Turtle Island* (New York: New Directions, 1974), p. 108.

ers, and trees of this living planet. We must also keep in mind the rights of future generations. The situation is grave. Our hope lies with those friends of the Earth all over the world who are rallying to her defense.

Chapter Three
Thinking Green!

*"Never doubt that a small group of thoughtful,
committed citizens can change the world. Indeed, it's
the only thing that ever has."* —Margaret Mead

When we founded the West German Green Party, we used the term "anti-party party" to describe our approach to politics based on a new understanding of power, a "counter-power" that is natural and common to all, to be shared by all, and used by all for all. This is the power of transformation, rooted in the discovery of our own strength and ability to be active participants in society. This kind of power stands in stark contrast to the power of domination, terror, and oppression, and is the best remedy for powerlessness.

Using power to dominate humans and nature has brought us to an impasse and can never take us beyond it. We must learn to think and act from our hearts, to recognize the interconnectedness of all living creatures, and to respect the value of each thread in the vast web of life. This is a spiritual perspective, and it is the foundation of all Green politics. It entails the radical, nonviolent transformation of the structures of society and of our way of thinking, so that domination is no longer the primary *modus operandi*. At the root of all Green political action is nonviolence, starting with how we live our lives, taking small, unilateral steps towards peace in everything we do. Green politics requires us to be both tender and subversive. Affirming tenderness as a political value is already subversive. In Green politics, we practice tenderness in relations with others; in caring for ideas, art, language, and culture; and in cherishing and protecting the Earth. To think Green is to build solidarity with those working for social justice and human rights everywhere, not bound by ideologies. The problems that threaten life on Earth were produced collectively, they affect us collectively, and we must act collectively to change them. We cannot retreat into isolation. The Green vision of a just society is one in which economic, social, and individual rights are guaranteed and protected, and everyone is free from exploitation, violence, and oppression.

Politicians give speeches about these values while working to undermine them. The benefits of the current political and economic systems are reserved for the privileged; therefore, any meaningful movement for social justice must focus on systemic change, on transforming both the oppressive state and economic structures that concentrate wealth and power in the hands of a few. The Green methodology is not to work from the top down, but to begin at the grassroots, empowering ourselves to direct our own destinies through the cultivation of civil space and democratic social forms.

First and foremost, Green politics is grassroots politics. Politics from the top is almost always corrupt and compromised. To bring about change from below is to challenge the moral authority of those who make decisions on our behalf. Through grassroots organization, education, and empowerment, we work to reverse the state-orientation of politics and instead open up a civil space in which we are active subjects, not passive objects of those in power. Substantive change in politics at the top will come only when there is enough pressure from below. The essence of Green politics is to live our values. We in the West German Green Party hurt ourselves over and over again by failing to maintain tenderness with each other as we gained power. We need to rededicate ourselves to our values, respect each other, be tolerant of differences, and stop trying to coerce and control one another.

Nonviolence, ecology, social justice, and feminism are the key principles of Green politics, and they are inseparably linked. We know, for example, that the wasteful patterns of production and consumption in the industrial North deplete and ravage the environment and furnish the motive and means for the violent appropriation of materials from the weaker nations in the South and for the wasteful process of militarization throughout the world. In both capitalist and state socialist countries, human beings are reduced to economic entities, with little or no regard for the human or ecological costs. Politics from the top, the pattern of hierarchical domination, is the characteristic of patriarchy. It is not a coincidence that power rests in the hands of men, benefits accrue first and foremost to men, and that women are exploited at all levels of society.

The Green approach to politics is a kind of celebration. We recognize that each of us is part of the world's problems, and we are also part of the solution. The dangers and the potentials for healing are not just outside us. We begin to work exactly where we are. There is no need to wait until conditions become ideal. We can simplify our lives and live in ways that affirm ecological and humane values. Better conditions will come because we have begun.

We have found so many ways to think each other to death—neutron warheads, nuclear reactors, Star Wars defense systems, and many other methods of mass destruction. We are killing each other with our euphemisms and abstractions. In warfare, we accept the deaths of thousands and millions of people we call our "enemy." When we dehumanize people, devalue nature, and exalt narrowly defined self-interests, destruction is sure to follow. The healing of our planet requires a new way of thinking about politics and about life. At the heart of this is the understanding that all things are intimately interconnected in the complex web of life. It can therefore be said that the primary goal of Green politics is an inner revolution. Joanna Macy calls this "the greening of the self."[1]

Politics needs spirituality. The profound political changes we need in order to heal our planet will not come about through fragmented problem solving or intellectual analyses that overlook the deepest yearnings and intuitions of the heart. Some of my fellow Greens have maintained their dogmatic leftist perspectives and remain suspicious of spirituality, confusing it with organized religion. I share many of their criticisms of religious institutions, but I firmly disagree with their dismissing spiritual concerns and wisdom. The long work of bringing harmony to the Earth requires a holistic vision based on mature values and deep intuitions.

Today's politics are based on the mechanistic worldview that prefers assertion to integration, analysis over synthesis, rational knowledge over intuitive wisdom, competition over cooperation, and expansionism over conservation. A few new ideas are not enough. We need an entirely new way of thinking. As we begin to cultivate a rich inner life

---

[1] Joanna Macy, *World as Lover, World as Self* (Berkeley: Parallax Press, 1991), p. 183.

and experience our connection with all of life, we realize how little of what society tells us we need is actually important for our well-being. We must reduce consumption and not cooperate with any practices that harm the natural world or other humans. This is not a sacrifice. It is the way to sustain ourselves.

Green politics must address the spiritual vacuum of industrial society, the alienation that is pervasive in a society where people have grown isolated from nature and from themselves. We in the Greens must also address our own alienation. Our social structures shape this alienation, and they themselves are shaped by it. It is a vicious cycle, and our work of healing must address the whole process. We have forgotten our historical rootedness in an integrated way of life. We must learn from those cultures that have maintained their traditions of wisdom and harmony with nature—Australian Aborigines, American Indians, and others. Tragically, many of these societies are threatened by the same forces that threaten the environment. We must join them in their struggles to preserve their values and traditions.

One such endangered society, Tibet, has been ruthlessly exploited and its people violently oppressed. The exiled leader of the Tibetan people, His Holiness the Dalai Lama, is, for me, a living example of how spiritual vision can influence politics:

> Peace starts within each one of us. When we have inner peace, we can be at peace with those around us. When our community is in a state of peace, it can share that peace with neighboring communities.... What is important is that we each make a sin-

cere effort to take seriously our responsibility for each other and for the natural environment.[2]

We have little reason to place our hope in governments or established political parties, for their primary interest is always in extending their own power. But we can find hope in the strength and imagination of people working at the grassroots to create positive change. We Greens work within the political system solely for the benefit and empowerment of those at the grassroots. Our efforts within the halls of government are not to replace work at the grassroots. Our commitments are, first and foremost, to those who elected us. We must work with them, nonviolently, for life-affirming solutions to the problems of our day.

Green politics is based on direct democracy—our effort is to redefine and reorganize power so that it flows from the bottom up. We seek to decentralize power and maximize the freedom and self-determination of individuals, communities, and societies. This means moving power out of the hands of centralized bureaucracies—above all, the military-industrial complex—and empowering people on the local level. It also means reaching across national borders and ideologies to build alliances with others also working for peace and ecology. It means moving government power away from the state towards smaller and smaller units of organization. In economics, grassroots democracy means a production system that maximizes workers' self-management and minimizes corporate or government control. It means units of production scaled to a comprehensible human dimension and that are lo-

---

[2] The Dalai Lama, "The Nobel Peace Prize Lecture," in *A Policy of Kindness* (Ithaca: Snow Lion Publications, 1990), p. 19.

cally responsive and globally responsible. The day may come when the Greens find a truly democratic and ecological partner among the established political parties, but until then, we must work in government as an anti-party party, an experiment in radical parliamentary opposition unwilling to compromise fundamental values for the sake of expediency.

Thinking green—to think with the heart—is the solution to many if not all of our political dead-ends. To continue increasing production, consumption, and the depletion of our natural resources will only lead us further down the path of suffering. Albert Einstein said that with the splitting of the atom everything changed except the way people think. A new way of thinking must come soon, or the damage will be irreparable. Means and ends cannot be separated. "There is no way to peace. Peace is the way."[3]

---

[3] A. J. Muste, *The Essays of A.J. Muste*, edited by Nat Hentoff (New York: Simon & Schuster, 1970).

Chapter Four

The Mega-Insanity of the Arms Race

"The whole world is a Hiroshima which the Bomb has not yet hit. The decision lies with all of us whether humanity must die together or whether it can live together." —R. Moritaki

These are troubled times. Even as the world is realigning itself following the end of the Cold War, arsenals all around the world, nuclear and so-called conventional, continue to grow and become more and more sophisticated. The arms race is the most immediate threat to our health, safety, and sanity.

The immense sums spent on manufacturing and storing weapons are nothing less than embezzlement by the leaders of the big nations and their wealthy backers. The discrepancy between the extravagant overproduction of armaments and the unsatisfied needs of those in developing countries and those marginalized by our affluent societies represent criminal aggression against the victims. Even when no one uses these new weapons, their very cost is killing us. And the philosophy of deterrence, still the norm of international relations, is a form of collective hysteria and blackmail.

The 1946 Nuremberg Trials ushered in a new era in international law permitting the prosecution of crimes against peace, war crimes, and crimes against humanity. The sentences handed down attempted to make the responsible political and military leaders of Germany accountable in law and to make them atone for their misdeeds. Statesmen and generals could no longer assume that their actions would simply be tolerated. Statesmen must be dedicated to preserving peace and upholding human rights and human dignity.

But the ideal of a legal order in which aggressors are accountable under international law has not been realized. Since World War II, hundreds of wars have been unleashed before our eyes and many obscene crimes committed against humanity. The passions aroused at the 1946 proceedings subsided by the early 1950s, and discussions among legal experts came to an end.

Now, the twentieth century is drawing to a close, and warfare has taken on a new character. The victims of our weapons are no longer visible to the perpetrators, and their pangs of death are no longer audible. You just press a button, open the bomb-doors, and release a bomb. Killing has become completely impersonal. Auschwitz and Hiroshima—the terrors of the twentieth century—show to what extremes human beings dare to go.

Edward Teller, the father of the hydrogen bomb, said that the most terrible thing about the current "false views" against nuclear strategy is that they unnecessarily increase the fears and suffering of the survivors:

> Let us take the extreme case that 5,000 nuclear weapons with an explosive force of between one and twenty megatons were detonated in the atmosphere. That would presumably reduce the ozone layer over the Northern Hemisphere of the Earth by 50 percent for a whole year. However, this would regenerate itself to 80 percent of its normal strength within a few years...[so] one can take it for granted that the human race could survive.[1]

---

[1] Interview in *Reader's Digest*, December 1982.

Teller's nuclear deterrence strategy is no less than mega-insanity. To defend freedom, we must be willing to destroy all of life. We have atomic shelters complete with aspirins and salami, even though no one would be able to reach these shelters in an emergency. Scientists study the choice between sudden death in an atomic holocaust and gradual ecological suicide. When faced with the knowledge that we are about to destroy ourselves, our minds switch off.

We must break the conspiracy of silence! As long as nuclear weapons exist anywhere on Earth, a nuclear war is probable, and we will destroy all that we are trying to protect. Deterrence thinking requires a willingness to perpetrate the very worst in order to prevent evil from triumphing. An absolute weapon presupposes an absolute enemy. Weapons of mass destruction supplant any possibility of practical politics.

Referring to the stand taken by the American Catholic bishops against nuclear weapons, "futurist" Hermann Kahn said, "Because of their immense influence and great prestige, the churches must be willing to abjure technical and strategic opinions that are unproven or simply false, but which sound good. In my view, the critical question is: when is it immoral to place our national security interests at risk because of some abstract or emotional concept of higher values." [2] We in the Greens greatly welcomed the stand of the American bishops, and also the initiatives of Anglican Bishop John Caker and his colleagues who declared that the possession of atomic weapons is neither justifiable in strategic terms nor compatible with Chris-

---

[2] *Die Welt am Sonntag,* December 19, 1982.

tian morality.[3] Cardinal Joseph Konig declared, "We believe that nothing could morally justify the death and destruction as would be caused by the use of atomic bombs. We reject the allegation that one side could win a nuclear war...."

In 1982, the West German Greens held a Tribunal in Nuremberg to try all of the governments that possess nuclear weapons for international war crimes. It is clear that every one of these weapons of mass destruction is illegal, as is the threat to use them. We drafted indictments, invited an international jury of legal experts and political scientists, and demanded "the worldwide denunciation of all politicians, scientists, military strategists, and technicians who plan, establish, pursue, or support techniques such as weapons systems designed for mass destruction and genocide." One New York attorney said, "We must assert international law before the event takes place if we wish to survive. There will be no Nuremberg Tribunal passing judgment on crimes against humanity after an atomic war because there will be no winners."[4]

We indicted the governments of West Germany, the United States, the Soviet Union, Great Britain, France, China, India, as well as all states that secretly possessed atomic weapons. Their willingness to have and therefore potentially to use atomic weapons removes the very foundations of international law and human rights. Their threat to use such weapons infringes upon the general rules of international law. They have not observed their accepted obligations to effect nuclear disarmament. The advances in weapons technology without any political con-

---

[3] "The Church and the Bomb," February 12-13, 1983.
[4] *Die Zeit* (No. 24/82).

trols make an atomic war inevitable and thus nullify the fundamental right enjoyed by all living and future human beings to their existence and security. At the end of the Tribunal, the jury decided that the indictments drawn up by the Greens were justified. We asked the accused states to give an account of themselves, but none sent an official representative. Governments must begin to observe international law. Those who committed murder in Southeast Asia with napalm are honored for having killed, while those who put up nonviolent resistance are declared criminals. Where justice becomes injustice, nonviolent resistance is our duty.

In the early 1980s, the Western European and American peace movements had a phase of massive mobilization in the capitals of Europe and America. Once a year, 300,000 or 500,000 of us or more came to parks and meadows and demonstrated nonviolently, although often with little creativity to dare more. Some of us also tried direct action projects to halt the deployment of new weapons: civil disobedience at military bases, war tax resistance, and so forth. But these actions represented only a small segment of the peace movement. Gert Bastian and I, who participated in many nonviolent sit-ins in front of military bases and were given very high fines, found ourselves more and more isolated within the Greens because of our participation in such nonviolent actions. I regret that we did not have enough courage to blockade the German defense ministry even more frequently, not only with fifty or a hundred people, but with 100,000 or 200,000 people. We needed more ongoing dialogue with police and soldiers to convince them that they should be our allies in nonviolence. Social defense has to include everyone.

Among German Greens, the debate in the 1980s concentrated on getting rid of Pershing II and Cruise Missiles. Many of us also tried to include on the agenda the SS-20s and other Soviet mass destructive weapons, and to add social, nonmilitary defense to our platform. But we were opposed by dogmatic Marxists who wanted to limit the debate to the lowest common denominator, simply arguing against American missiles in Western Europe. They also opposed our solidarity with the independent peace movements in Eastern Europe, urging instead cooperation with the governmentally run "peace councils."

On November 21, 1986, together with Gert Bastian and other friends, I sat in front of the NATO building site in Hasselbach, in the Hunsrück Mountains, where U.S. intermediate-range cruise missiles were to be deployed. We sat in the pouring rain in front of an entrance to the building site, sang, and had discussions with the police. Although we offered no resistance whatsoever, in just a few minutes we were hauled away by the police and charged "with having broken the law…through joint action, by forcing others to act, tolerating action by others, or refraining from acting." They called our objective "reprehensible," and they equated our nonviolent sit-in with violence. Reprehensible means "morally objectionable," "amoral," something "to be rejected because of social ethics." According to judgments handed down by West German courts, Tolstoy, Gandhi, Jesus, and Martin Luther King all acted in a reprehensible manner.

It is ironic that nonviolent actions in front of military sites on which weapons of mass destruction are stored are punishable offenses. The question of whether symbolic sit-ins really constitute violence should be discussed openly and honestly. Is it really coercion to encourage, through this kind of symbolic action, public debate about a development that is practically irreversible, one that means that 40,000 children have to die every day? Many people throughout the world have participated in nonviolent campaigns against weapons of mass destruction, and these actions have helped bring about some disarmament agreements between the superpowers. Can these nonviolent actions be considered coercion or violence? Are they really reprehensible? The deployment of missiles and the massive buildup of arms is an issue of vital importance for all humanity.

When German truck drivers organized blockades that obstructed the flow of traffic to a far greater extent than all the nonviolent sit-ins of the peace movement taken together, in most cases no charges were filed. These were nonviolent actions, organized within the framework of a strategy pursued by the trade union movement, and yet no criminal proceedings were initiated because, as the Interior Minister of North Rhine-Westphalia put it, "The jobs of 50,000 people are at stake." The nonviolent actions of the peace movement are concerned with the survival of millions of people, and yet, for these actions, we have been tried in court and sentenced. Sit-ins of two, three, and five minutes are considered criminal offenses, while blockades lasting several hours at borders and traffic intersections are not. Reality has been turned upside down. Weapons of mass destruction that threaten the lives of millions of people are considered morally acceptable, even peaceful, while we who participate in peaceful demonstrations in front of missile bases are regarded as violent. Astronomical arms budgets and arms exports are killing people in the Third World. We must speak the truth. The truth involves understanding the motives of those who nonviolently protest the arms buildup, and it involves understanding why those responsible for the military and nuclear buildup that could result in the destruction of all forms of life are not being tried and convicted as criminals.

Countries and individuals resort to violence much too quickly. The ideology of violence and the threat of mutual destruction define our national and personal security policies. When there is a political or a military crisis anywhere in the world, we accept the idea that force and murder are appropriate means at the disposal of the state. At the end of such conflicts, the parties involved allegedly make peace and forget about the mass graves that cover the Earth. Governments and military chiefs know nothing about nonmilitary forms of defense and have little interest in learning about them. It is up to us in the peace movement to find a way out of the insane strategy of mutual destruction. We must refuse to submit to thinking in terms of violence.

In a nonviolent action, people must not be threatened or injured. During many nonviolent actions, I have talked with servicemen and servicewomen who work on missile bases, engaging in dialogue with them over the fences. I have spoken with policemen, many of whom were also convinced that nonviolence is the only possible course. I especially remember discussions I had with policemen in the pouring rain in front of the NATO building site in November 1986. These were constructive talks that showed me how well many policemen understand our commitment.

Many of our Green analyses and predictions have proven correct, and many of our ideas have been widely adopted. But we must not forget that our approach and

our understanding are by no means the norm. To quote
from a brochure published by the West German Ministry
of Defense:

> The purpose of nuclear weapons is primarily politi-
> cal, namely to prevent war through deterrence in
> peacetime and, if this is not successful, to end a mili-
> tary conflict as rapidly as possible by threatening to
> use these weapons or making limited use of them
> under political control. Political control of the use
> of nuclear weapons is guaranteed at all times.[5]

In this brochure, the Defense Minister publicly admits
that Cruise Missiles with nuclear warheads ten times more
powerful than the atomic bomb dropped on Hiroshima
could be used to bring about a rapid end to a war. The
deployment of weapons of mass destruction, the effect of
which no one can imagine, is regarded as legal, while the
symbolic obstruction of the deployment of these weapons,
carried out in a nonviolent way by people concerned only
about the future of humanity, is called a "reprehensible
act of violence" under the rule of law.

Under the West German Constitution, we can refuse
to serve in a war effort on grounds of conscience. But a
nuclear, chemical, or conventional war can be prepared
and unleashed at the push of a button or by a computer,
so what can refusing to serve mean? We must refuse now
by opposing all arms buildups and arms exports. Each of
us bears personal responsibility at a time when weapons
of mass destruction, as well as other types of very smart
weapons are being increasingly perfected. We know that
in the minds of the military chiefs, deterrence makes sense

---

[5] "Cruise Missiles in the Hunsrück Mountains," brochure, 1986.

only if the other side knows that this is no idle threat and that nuclear weapons will be unleashed if the conflict escalates beyond a certain point. What could be a more bizarre "security" policy?

Many of us carry in our hearts the words of Sophie Scholl, a member of the resistance movement who was executed by the Nazis: "Tear up the cloak of indifference that you have wrapped around your hearts! Make up your minds before it is too late!" It is not too late yet. I hope people will come to understand why we in the Greens protest against the arms race so strongly. We do so in the spirit of a higher law, a law in favor of life. Our aim is nothing less than the abolition of all weapons and the disbanding of all military armies. It is time for us to put all our resources and energies into peace. Tomorrow may be too late.

Chapter Five
Nonviolent Social Defense

*"People try nonviolence for a week, and when it
'doesn't work,' they go back to violence, which hasn't
worked for centuries."* —Theodore Roszak

Young people are our future. It is they who can become
peacemakers in their lives and develop a nonviolent future. We must encourage them to study peace and to challenge the military-industrial complex that continues to
push us into wars and ever-expanding military budgets.
The study of peace analyzes the causes of war, violence,
and systematic oppression, and explores the processes by
which conflict and change can be managed in order to
maximize justice and minimize violence. Peace studies
encompass the fields of economics, politics, history, political science, physics, ethics, philosophy, and religion at
the local as well as global levels, showing how culture, ideology, and technology relate to conflict and change.

War, peace, and justice are the most critical issues we
face today, and they must receive the highest priority. It is
important that students debate peace issues and design
research projects on how to conclude arms control treaties, how to initiate steps toward unilateral disarmament,
and how to protect human rights wherever they are violated. We will not find an instant solution to the nearly
half-century of nuclear buildup, so we must make a sustained effort to undertake peace research, action research,
and analysis.

Peace studies should also touch the spirituality of politics, talking about the problems of poverty, oppression, and the nature of war, and offering alternatives to war, militarism, and deterrence. Peace studies programs can help develop, through action research, practical methods for the nonviolent resolution of conflicts, including civilian-based defense and social defense. It should also discuss Third World development, ecological planning, human rights, social movements, and grassroots movements. A peace studies program should convey the development of the civil rights and antiwar movements and evaluate the powerful effects of these movements. Students who become involved in looking for nonviolent solutions to military conflicts are on the way to becoming true peacemakers. We need many students to become peacemakers if we want to have hope for the future.

Human dignity is a fundamental value in peace education. Innovative learning to prepare people to act conscientiously in situations in which issues of right or wrong are at stake is sorely needed. This means moving away from the emphasis on competition, achievement, strength, power, profit, and productivity. Peace studies must guide students toward active global citizenship and solving conflicts nonviolently, and must help them acquire the capacity to confront changes and use their personal influence to bring about positive change. Peace studies can, I hope, become truly peacemaking—helping develop an ethic of reverence for life on this Earth, a planet that has no emergency exit. Improving the human social condition is part of peacemaking. I wish our young students the strength and courage to become real peacemakers. The immense task of students and educators is no less than the survival of our planetary home.

"Wars will end when people refuse to fight," expresses the Green approach to peace. The cornerstone of this approach is unilateral disarmament. It is a completely new principle of foreign policy, breaking with the spurious logic of the balance of power and the limits of diplomatic exchange which leads to continual militarism. To embark on a unilateral, nonaligned, and actively neutral departure from the entire military system is to initiate a policy of nonthreatening conduct essential for any real security or peace.

We Greens want to create the conditions for this new way to peace that is completely without the use of military force. Almost everyone in the world thinks that deterrence thinking, stereotypes of the enemy, and belief in the inevitability of war are the only practical ways of operating. But the abolition of slavery once seemed unrealistic, and the abolition of arms, too, can become the norm in international affairs. A disarmed society need not be defenseless. Civilian-based social defense is an alternative to the self-destructive militarism that has been tried again and again and has only brought us more and more suffering. It is time for a fresh new approach, one that is studied and documented and not just naive.

One of the most important advocates of civilian-based defense is Gene Sharp, of the Albert Einstein Institution in Cambridge, Massachusetts. Professor Sharp has studied nonviolent defense worldwide, and has seen that this is a practical and effective strategy, based on the recognition that power derives, first and foremost, from the consent of the governed. Civilian-based defense depends on the highly skilled, coordinated resistance of citizens.

During the Summer of 1968, when nonviolent citizens in Prague were resisting the occupying Soviet forces, my grandmother and I were there in a hotel near Wenceslaus Square, under house arrest. Even after Dubcek and his close associates were arrested, the people remained steadfast in their resistance. Eventually, by threatening indefinite military occupation, the Soviets were able to reassert their authority and delay the reforms of the Prague Spring by twenty-one years. But through their sacrifice and suffering, the people of Czechoslovakia built up a spirit of positive patriotism, and two decades later did indeed succeed in their "Velvet Revolution." These events demonstrate the power of nonviolent social defense.

Social defense is a way to protect ourselves from foreign invasions or internal *coups* through active, nonviolent resistance and noncooperation, including economic boycotts by consumers and producers, social and political boycotts of institutions, strikes, overtaking facilities and administrative systems important to the opponent, stalling and obstructing, being deliberately inefficient, ostracizing, influencing occupying troops, and other forms of not complying. Military defense seeks to prevent an enemy from invading by threatening battle losses at the border. Social defense sets an unacceptably high price on staying—ceaseless resistance. It spoils the spoils of war and deprives the aggressor of the fruits of victory. The price of aggression becomes so high that occupation is no longer worth it. The opponent is prevented from attaining their aims and their ability to fight is undermined.

Social defense is practical and pragmatic. It requires excellent preparation, organization, and training; a courageous, creative, and determined citizenry; and a radical commitment to democratic values. Independent, resourceful, freedom-loving people that are prepared and organized to resist aggression cannot be conquered. No number of tanks and missiles can dominate a society unwilling to cooperate. In this century, we have seen several examples of the effectiveness of nonviolent social defense. The home-rule movement led by Gandhi mobilized so much grassroots pressure that the British were forced to withdraw from India. The civil rights movement created profound changes in U.S. society. Philippine "people power" overthrew Marcos nonviolently. And in Eastern Europe, it was citizens' movements, not political or military powers, that toppled the state security systems.

Full demilitarization can only come about in a society in which power is shared at the grassroots. In the nineteenth century, Henry David Thoreau called upon free citizens to engage in civil disobedience and nonviolent actions whenever there is injustice. Civil disobedience and nonviolence are an integral part of any democratic society. Even in Western democracies, the state seems invincible, and as individuals we often feel powerless, unable to have much effect. We must remind ourselves that the power of the state derives solely from the consent of the governed. Without the cooperation of the people, the state cannot exist. Even a powerful military state that is nearly invulnerable to violent force can be transformed through nonviolence at the grassroots. Noncooperation, civil disobedience, education, and organization are the means of change, and we must learn the ways to use them. Direct democracies will come into being only when we demand from our leaders that they listen to us. This is fundamental to Green politics. Power is not something that we receive from above. To transform our societies into ones that are peaceful, ecological, and just, we need only to exercise the power we already have.

Like the militaristic mode of defense, social defense demands courage and the willingness to place the interests of the community ahead of individual self-interest, relying as it does on well-organized, tightly bonded affinity groups in every neighborhood prepared to conduct acts of nonviolent resistance on short notice. Every neighborhood must know how to conduct resistance and subversion. This method of democratic security requires little material apparatus but a lot of organization and training.

It is easy to see how economically wasteful, ecologically destructive, immoral, and counter-democratic military defense is, but to criticize militarism is not enough. If we really want to move towards nonviolent societies, we must study and begin to practice some alternatives, and civilian-based defense is the most realistic and effective.

The very fabric of every First World country is woven by militarism. The culture of materialism depends on the use of force. Violence, oppression, and domination are all ways used by the powerful to keep the powerless powerless. In capitalist societies, the social structure depends on the economic exploitation of one group by another, in the form of imperialism abroad and racism at home. Violence is inherent and pervasive, from the nuclear family to the nuclear state.

As long as the world is divided into centralized states in competition for material wealth and political power, war is inevitable, as is the domination of weaker states by stronger ones. SS-20s, Pershing IIs, Tridents, Star Wars "defense" systems, and other weapons do not begin in factories. They begin in our consciousness. We think each other to death. The entire production cycle—from the allocation of funds, to the mining of uranium, to testing—is killing people. American Indian children playing on their reservation lands are breathing radioactive tailings from the waste piles of uranium mines. The radiation poisoning of Pacific Islanders is the result of weapons testing by the French government. Every year, while hundreds of billions of dollars go toward preparation for war, seventeen million children under the age of five die of starvation or inadequate medical care.

The destruction of nature, the militarization of the world, and the exploitation of the disenfranchised all kill life and kill the spirit. We "shut down" and not only numb our fear and pain, we also lose touch with our own innate spiritual resources—compassion, imagination, and the power to respond. As Joanna Macy points out, it is precisely because of our caring, our compassion, and our recognition of our connectedness with life that the pain of the world is so unbearable.[1] These are the qualities that we need most to bring change and healing to our world. We must reclaim our spiritual power.

Satyagraha, "truth force," is the word used by Gandhi to describe the spiritual power of nonviolence. *Ahimsa,* "non-harming," is a value deeply embedded in the Indian religious outlook that shaped Gandhi's thought. The power of nonviolence arises from what is deepest and most humane within ourselves and speaks directly to what is deepest and most humane in others. Nonviolence works not through defeating the opponent but by awakening the opponent and oneself through openness. It is not just a tactic—it embraces life. "Nonviolence that merely offers civil resistance to the authorities and goes no further scarcely deserves the name ahimsa," Gandhi said. "To quell riots nonviolently, there must be true ahimsa in one's

---

[1] Joanna Macy, *World as Lover,* pp. 15-28.

heart, an ahimsa that takes even the erring hooligan in its warm embrace."[2]

In acknowledging Gandhi's influence, Dr. Martin Luther King, Jr. made this point: "I had about concluded that the ethics of Jesus were only effective in individual relationships. The 'turn the other cheek' philosophy and the 'love your enemies' philosophy were only valid, I felt, when individuals were in conflict with other individuals; when racial groups and nations were in conflict, a more realistic approach seemed necessary. But after reading Gandhi, I saw how utterly mistaken I was. Gandhi was probably the first person in history to lift the love ethic of Jesus above mere interaction between individuals to a powerful and effective social force on a large scale."[3] Nonviolence extends moral thought beyond individuals and their immediate communities to include the whole of society. It takes the initiative in opposing existing systems of dominance and privilege and addresses the problem of structural violence and the task of structural change.

Faith that we have a natural disposition to love, that we are possessed of moral conscience, and that all life is sacred are at the foundation of nonviolent action, and we can see their power in practical application. The political techniques of nonviolence—noncooperation, civil disobedience, grassroots organizing, fasting, and so forth—derive their power from the faith and confidence that through the integrity and self-sacrifice of our actions, we can awaken our opponent's conscience and bring about a change of heart. Gandhi was uniquely creative in apply-

---

[2] Mohandas K. Gandhi, *The Story of My Experiments with Truth* (Boston: Beacon Press, 1957).

[3] Martin Luther King, Jr., *Stride Toward Freedom: The Montgomery Story* (New York: Harper & Brothers, 1958), pp. 96-97.

ing nonviolence as an effective force for political and social change. For him, nonviolence was always active, powerful, and dynamic, and had nothing to do with passivity or acceptance of wrongful conditions. He acknowledged the influence of the nineteenth century Indian women's movement in the development of his approach. Because women's contributions to nonviolence are often unrecognized, this influence is especially encouraging. He was also directly influenced by Jesus' gospel of love and the writings of Tolstoy, Emerson, and Thoreau.

Violence always leads to more violence, hatred to greater hatred. Nonviolence works through communion, never through coercion. We must win over, not defeat, our opponent through openness, dialogue, patience, and love. Our real opponent is not a human enemy, but a system and way of thinking that give some people the power to oppress. Each struggle is part of a larger vision, one of building a society dedicated to the welfare of all. Gandhi felt that India could only become healthy with strong, politically autonomous, economically self-reliant villages. He was critical of industrialism for dehumanizing workers, splitting society into classes, and taking work from humans and giving it to machines. And he saw that any centralized production system requires a state that is restrictive of individual freedom. To him, the spinning wheel represented the dignity of labor, self-sufficiency, and humility needed to guide the people of India in the work of social transformation. Gandhi's influence runs deep in the Green movement. Satyagraha and all it implies have inspired and informed our vision of nonviolent change.

All forms of structural and institutional violence—the arms race, warfare, economic deprivation, social injustice, ecological exploitation, and so forth—are closely linked.

Making their interrelationships clear is essential for moving society in a direction that benefits all, not just one nation, class, or even species. Militarism and the culture of militarism are extreme and pervasive examples of structural violence, even in times of relative peace. People assume that militarism at least boosts our economies. But defense spending generates fewer jobs than other areas of public spending. "It produces," as Jesse Jackson has pointed out, "little of utility to our society—no food, no clothes, no housing, no medical equipment or supplies. In short, nothing of social or redemptive value."[4] For the cost of just one jet fighter, 3 million children could be inoculated against major childhood diseases. The cost of one nuclear weapons test could provide enough money to give 80,000 Third World villages access to safe water through the installation of hand pumps. Two billion dollars are spent every day on military weapons. Contrasted with the urgent needs of the world's poor, military expenditures are nothing short of embezzlement.

The ending of the Cold War has brought little change in our militaristic outlook. As old weapons systems are dismantled, they are replaced by new, more sophisticated ones. Weapons research and development continues unabated. Militaries, the arms industry, government leaders, and bureaucrats continue to tell citizens that more refined weapons in larger numbers will bring greater security, and sales of arms and weapons technology continue worldwide.

A nation's policies, values, institutions, and structures comprise the preconditions for violence or for peace. Gandhi said, "Nonviolence is the greatest force mankind

---

[4] Rev. Jesse L. Jackson, *Straight from the Heart* (Philadelphia: Fortress Press, 1987), p. 283.

has ever been endowed with. Love has more force than a besieging army." Martin Luther King, Jr. added that this power of love is physically passive but spiritually active— that "while the non-violent resister is passive in the sense that he is not physically aggressive towards his opponent, his mind and his emotions are constantly active, constantly seeking to persuade the opposition." Nonviolence is a spiritual weapon that can succeed where guns and armies never could. "Democracy can only be saved through non-violence," Gandhi said, "because democracy, so long as it is sustained by violence, cannot provide for or protect the weak. My notion of democracy is that under it the weakest should have the same opportunity as the strongest. This can never happen except through nonviolence."

Now, when the West has more or less won the Cold War, the Warsaw Pact has completely crumbled and NATO is about to move its borders east, a pragmatic, nonideological approach to social defense must be developed and counterposed to all militaristic policies. We spend billions on weapons research and millions training our young people at military academies. Why not invest in peace studies and peace actions? We need training centers, public campaigns, and educational materials. We need to support groups like Peace Brigades International that intervene nonviolently in situations of conflict. We need to work concretely to realize peace and nonviolence in our time.

We also need to support existing nonviolent struggles, such as those of the Tibetans and the Chinese democracy movement. The public is so often ignorant about these nonviolent campaigns, because bombing oneself into history like the IRA, ETA, and others is what receives media and public attention. We can never give peace a chance if we do not even know about the many peaceful movements already in existence.

There are a few hopeful signs. In 1989, 36 percent of the Swiss population voted against having an army, and, though underfunded, small-scale feasibility studies on the same subject were done in Sweden, Denmark, Holland, Austria, and France. I hope that all peace groups will take up the issue of social defense as a main priority. Gandhi said, "Nonviolence is as yet a mixed affair. It limps. Nevertheless, it is there and it continues to work like a leaven in a silent and invisible way, least understood by most. [But] it is the only way."

Chapter Six

Human Rights
Cannot Be Compromised

*"We are caught in a network of mutuality, tied in a single
garment of destiny. Whatever affects one directly, affects us
all indirectly."* —Martin Luther King, Jr. [1]

In 1983, while appearing on "Meet the Press," I expressed
shock at the Reagan administration's double standard on
issues of human rights. It denounced Nicaragua as a "totalitarian superpower" to justify military intervention, yet
when asked about human rights abuses in allied countries
like Chile, Guatemala, and Turkey, the administration
counseled "patience," another word for doing nothing.
But what shocked me most was how the questions of the
show's reporters were completely framed by the same Cold
War mentality. They were not the least bit interested in
discussing human rights, only whether I was more sympathetic to the Soviet Union or the U.S. When I told them
that many of us in Europe felt threatened by the buildup
of the U.S. nuclear arsenal in West Germany, the reporters' main concern was whether the U.S.S.R. made me feel
equally threatened. They were unable to imagine how one
could base one's political views on anything other than
the rivalry of the superpowers. By keeping the discussion
within the framework of the Cold War, they prevented any
critical examination of the U.S. or Western Europe.

---

[1] "A Christmans Sermon on Peace," from J.M. Washington, ed., *A Testament
of Hope: The Essential Writings of Martin Luther King, Jr.* (San Francisco:
Harper & Row, 1986), p. 254.

Washington officials and reporters either could not or would not discuss things from the premise that any commitment to peace, social justice, and human rights must be principled and consistent, and they are hardly unique. When we look around the world, we see countless, unspeakable ways that basic human rights are violated and little moral consistency on the part of governments in addressing this. Concern with human rights is too often simply a matter of expedience, rhetoric, economic interests, or geopolitical strategy.

Peace, justice, and human rights cannot be for some and not for others, and commitment to their realization cannot be dictated by state interests. The state is not absolute, and loyalty to the state cannot be absolute. Loyalty toward each other and toward the whole of life is far more important than any ideology, political system, boundary, border, or military alliance.

Martin Luther King spoke of the inseparability of human rights, social justice, and peace. When he announced his opposition to the U.S. war in Vietnam, he was sharply criticized by many of his supporters who felt he was hurting the civil rights movement by taking an unpopular stand on a "tangential" issue. But he refused to sacrifice moral integrity for tactical expediency. Instead, he showed the clear links between militarism abroad and racism at home, between economic exploitation and social oppression. He knew that violence, oppression, and domination are ways to keep the powerful powerful and the powerless powerless, that there can be no peace while one race dominates another, while one people, one nation, or one sex despises another. Human rights are indivisible. Any violation anywhere is everyone's responsibility.

By social justice, I mean those conditions under which individuals and communities can determine their own lives and destinies and under which they can grow to their full potential. Any society that aspires to be just must be structured upon basic guarantees and protections of its citizens' safety and freedom. Societies may vary in the forms through which justice and rights are put into practice, but as principles they must remain primary, guiding values. Everyone everywhere has the right to be safe from violence and free from state intrusion, social oppression, and economic and political exploitation. And everyone has the right to work to make these ideals a reality.

The Western democracies generally invoke their moral obligation to safeguard human rights only when their strategic or political interests are affected. When their interests are not at stake, they tend to remain silent, avert their eyes from unpleasant realities, use "quiet" (and usually ineffective) diplomacy, and they justify this attitude with the spurious argument that intervention in the internal affairs of another state is not permissible. The principle of nonintervention has been used for too long as an excuse to tolerate human rights violations and even genocide. In our global village of increasing interdependence, there can be no more shilly-shallying on this issue. There are entire peoples in jeopardy of extinction. We must do something about these abuses and not just leave them to be worked out between the perpetrators and the victims. These crimes concern the whole of the international community.

Intervention in a state's internal affairs is sometimes necessary to safeguard human rights. Repressive governments should not be able to claim with impunity that their abuses of human rights are purely internal matters, nor should other countries be able to hide behind the principle of nonintervention to justify their own inaction. It is the moral responsibility of the United Nations to expand its role beyond the mere defending of national borders. It is the UN's moral responsibility to meddle in the internal affairs of repressive regimes that violate the lives of those within their borders. But it is not only the UN's responsibility. Meddling on behalf of human rights is the responsibility of everyone. I am not speaking about the self-interested use of force to extend military and economic interests. I mean the nonaligned, universal, and nonviolent application of moral principles to international politics.

Meddling is an essential aspect of Green politics. During the years of the Cold War, many of us in the West German Greens advocated meddling in the internal human rights affairs of both military blocs, without allegiance to the White House or the Kremlin. We spoke out against the Soviet invasion of Afghanistan and against U.S. militarism in Central America and the Caribbean. We joined our East German friends in East Berlin's Alexanderplatz to demonstrate for peace and human rights. We demonstrated in Turkey against a military dictatorship accepted within the NATO alliance. And we demonstrated both in Moscow and in Washington, D.C. against the proliferation of nuclear arms.

But the record of the German Greens has not been unstained. One of the most painful experiences of my years as an activist was the abandonment by many Greens of the Tibetan people in their struggle against the genocidal policies of China. The Tibetans are indisputably a separate and distinct people from China. They inhabit a defined territory, the Tibetan plateau, where their unique culture has flourished for centuries. International attorney Michael van Walt writes, "Even if one were to accept China's argument that Tibet was in some way part of the Manchu emperors' dominions until 1911, there is no question but that Tibetans governed themselves for centuries with only occasional and minimal interference. From 1911 to 1949, Tibet conducted itself in every respect as an independent state."[2] The Chinese occupation of Tibet in 1949 was undertaken by force and against the wishes of the Tibetan people and their government.

Since the occupation, more than one million Tibetans have been killed. Hundreds of thousands have saved themselves only by fleeing the country. Through forced sterilizations and abortions on a massive scale, the Tibetan population is being even further diminished. Since 1983, China has been flooding Tibet with Han Chinese settlers so that today there are 160,000 Chinese living in Lhasa and only about 50,000 Tibetans. Tibetans are becoming a minority in their own country! They have been robbed of their centers of spiritual and religious life by the systematic destruction of almost all of their 5,000 monasteries. Disruption of the traditional balance between agriculture and livestock production has led to mismanagement and unprecedented famines. The ruthless exploitation of rich mineral resources, the destruction of wildlife and forests, the militarization of what was once a zone of peace in Central Asia, and its misuse as a dumping site for nuclear waste and the deployment of Chinese nuclear missiles are further landmarks in the merciless elimination of one of the oldest and most highly developed civilizations in the world.

---

[2] See *The Anguish of Tibet,* edited by Petra K. Kelly, Gert Bastian, and Pat Aiello (Berkeley: Parallax Press, 1991), pp. 60-64.

At the national Green Party conference in 1988, a motion calling for an international hearing on Tibet was opposed by many left-wing delegates who said that the Dalai Lama was an exploitative tyrant, that supporting the "backward" people of Tibet would mean accepting their religious and social structures, and that as an "atheistic" party we could not support a religious people. No one had ever suggested we ask how religious were the mothers of the Plaza de Mayo before giving them support. We never asked how often the people of Nicaragua went to Mass or how often the people of Chile took Holy Communion.

Despite this opposition, the motion for the conference was eventually carried, and a two-day hearing was held in April 1989 that succeeded in bringing together human rights experts, authorities on Tibet and China, representatives of the Tibetan government-in-exile, and eyewitnesses of some of the atrocities. Emerging from the meeting was the Tibet Appeal, which was signed by 6,000 people from around the world, and from which we received many donations to further work on behalf of Tibet. But even though just one month before the conference hundreds of Tibetans were massacred by Chinese soldiers during nonviolent demonstrations in Lhasa, many left-wing Greens were still not interested in signing the appeal, donating money, or even hearing further about the plight of the Tibetan people.[3]

Less than three months after the Tibet conference, on June 3, Chinese troops marched through Tiananmen Square, massacring unarmed, nonviolent pro-democracy demonstrators. For two months, the Chinese students, workers, and intellectuals had staged a historic nonviolent

---

[3] The proceedings of this conference, along with other documents regarding the genocide in Tibet, are in *The Anguish of Tibet.*

struggle for freedom and democracy. Representing the aspirations of the Chinese people, the movement had received broad-based support from all strata of society. The movement was not opposed to socialism, but rather called into question the political and material privileges enjoyed by an elite class of functionaries. During the many marches, sit-ins, and hunger strikes, the demonstrators adhered strictly to the principle of nonviolence in pressing to transform a dictatorship of a corrupt party into a socialist democracy. The crackdown that began in Tiananmen Square resulted in the imprisonment, harassment, torture, and murder of many thousands. Where there had been a movement of promise and hope, we witnessed state terror in its most complete form. As in the Moscow trials of the late 1930s, the East German workers' revolt in 1953, Hungary in 1956, Prague Spring of 1968, and the coup against Solidarity in 1981, revolutionary attempts at gaining freedom were denounced as "counterrevolutionary" and ruthlessly crushed.

The response of the West German Greens to these events, though greater than in the case of Tibet, was uncharacteristically tepid. This was generally true as well of the broader peace and progressive movements in Europe and the U.S. Press statements and resolutions condemning the bloodbath were issued, but we saw little of the solidarity, passion, and creativity we have seen in response to atrocities in El Salvador, Chile, South Africa, Afghanistan, or Eastern Europe. If 20,000 people were murdered in front of the White House or the Kremlin, the response would certainly have been different.

In the days and weeks following the crackdown in China, I heard many within the Greens and the peace movement say they condemned the massacre but found it difficult to understand the aims and demands of the pro-democracy movement. Some criticized the movement for not having a program, for being supported by Taiwanese students, or for being bourgeois. Some were sympathetic to the hollow claims of the ruling regime that China is a revolutionary state. But to be misled by such concerns betrays our principles and undermines our credibility. It betrays, as well, those who suffer under a brutal regime.

In the more than forty years since China invaded and annexed Tibet, the world has maintained a shameful silence. It is perhaps the Tibetan people's tragedy that their fate was not a part of the great East-West conflict. If it had been the Soviets, and not the Chinese, who had overpowered them, the occupation of their country would certainly have drawn the protests of the West. Certainly, if Tibet were a country rich in oil, like Kuwait, there would be serious pressure on Beijing to return Tibet's sovereignty. But it is the misfortune of the Tibetan people that there is no strategic or economic incentive to move the international community to action.

Our silence—the silence of the international community and the silence of the peace and progressive movements—is killing Tibet. If the world continues to stand by, the Tibetan people will not survive. The Green Party's hearing on Tibet was a first attempt at breaking through the silence, pressing for solidarity with the Tibetan people, and sparking strong international protest over China's policy. Our efforts were reinforced by conferences in New Delhi, Copenhagen, The Hague, Brussels, Dharamsala, Tokyo, and London. The awarding of the Nobel Peace Prize to the Dalai Lama in 1989 was a strong reminder to the world of the plight of Tibet. The courage shown by Czechoslovakian president Vaclav Havel in inviting the

Dalai Lama to Prague as the representative of an oppressed people, despite strong Chinese protests, put to shame all those Western heads of state who, out of deference to China, have painstakingly avoided all contact with the leader of the Tibetan people. Our deference must be replaced by demands for talks between Beijing and the Tibetan government-in-exile. Unrelentingly, consistently, and without concern for economic advantage, the world must demand that China display a willingness to find a solution to the question of Tibet, one that is based on tolerance, humaneness, and the right of the Tibetan people to self-determination. If we do not, Tibet will be lost to the world.

All over the world, in places like Indonesia, Borneo, the Amazon forest, Bolivia, Peru, Guatemala, parts of Central Africa, Australia, New Zealand, China, Tibet, and the former Soviet Union, native peoples trying to live in their traditional manner are suffering from the expansion of Western society and Western ways of life. There is at least one ray of hope—a new alternative United Nations which is called the Unrepresented Nations and Peoples Organization. UNPO is a nonaligned body dedicated to developing programs and solutions to the problems faced by minority groups, indigenous peoples, and occupied territories not officially recognized by the United Nations. Because the UN has been entirely ineffective in conflicts involving these forgotten peoples, UNPO has been established as a forum for ethnic minorities and nation peoples to express their grievances, exchange experiences, pool resources, and work together to create opportunities for diplomacy and dialogue between the UN, its member states, and those who are excluded.

The Universal Declaration of Human Rights, proclaimed by the United Nations General Assembly in 1948, made no provision for the protection of peoples living within the borders of recognized states. We have seen some movement on the part of the UN to protect the rights of indigenous peoples, but it is not nearly enough. The UN is rooted in and constrained by the outlook and interests of the powerful states. I attended the first UNPO meeting in The Hague, Netherlands, in August 1991. It was a good and hopeful feeling to sit with friends representing peoples forgotten by the international community of states: Kurds, Tibetans, American Indians, Australian Aborigines, native Hawaiians, members of the Greek minority in Albania, Armenians, and many others.

The plight of the Tibetan people is just one example of a worldwide crisis that many are not even aware of. "Nation peoples," distinct, socially integrated cultural groups living in traditionally defined territories, comprise one-third of the world's population. Their traditional territories are mostly within the borders of states, where they are marginalized, impoverished, and persecuted. Millions of other people are members of ethnic minorities, groups that are culturally distinct but without their own territory. Like nation people, they too are often oppressed and ignored. Throughout the world, we see policies of genocide on the part of states seeking to destroy distinct cultural groups. Genocide is the annihilation of a people, by either physical killing or the destruction of their culture. Its forms vary—military warfare, denial of basic rights, development policies that undermine the group's identity or way of life. The same kinds of brutal tactics employed by the Chinese in Tibet are used throughout the world.

UNPO links these oppressed peoples together in a forum for common action.

Ethnic minorities and nation peoples face many of the same tragic problems, but it is important to note one distinction. A common people living within its traditional territory is not a minority just because that territory has been annexed by a more powerful state. Yet throughout the world, nation peoples are referred to as ethnic minorities, thereby refuting their claim to self-determination, justifying the theft of their resources, or legitimizing their repression as an internal state matter.

In his essay "The Third World War," Bernard Nietschmann points out that, although we tend to use the terms interchangeably, the distinction between nations and states is vital. A nation is the geographically bounded territory of communities that see themselves as a single people based on common ancestry, history, language, territory, social forms, economic ties, religion, or ideology. A state is a centralized political system, recognized by other states, that uses a civilian and military bureaucracy to enforce one set of institutions, laws, and sometimes language and religion within its claimed boundaries. As Nietschmann shows, "States commonly claim many nations that may not consent to being governed and absorbed by an imposed central government in the hands of different people."

There are more than 175 internationally recognized states in the world, and there are more than three thousand nations, few of which are recognized or even heard of internationally. According to Nietschmann, of the more than one hundred armed conflicts being fought around the world, nearly three-quarters are between states and nations: Iraq and Kurdistan, Burma and the Karen people,

Israel and Palestinians, Syria and Palestinians, Indonesia and West Papua, Britain and Ulster, Guatemala and the Mayan people. The list goes on, the deaths and casualties are in the millions, yet few acknowledge the pattern of states imposing rule and absorbing the territories and resources of nations. Because nation peoples rarely have a voice in the international community, they often see no alternative to violent resistance to maintain their lives as a people.

These circumstances are even more tragic and lethal when powerful states supply arms to the combatants to further their own geopolitical interests and increase industrial profits. The fate of the Kurdish people is a case in point. Nietschmann tells us that the Kurds have at various times received assistance from the U.S.S.R., the U.S., Israel, and Iran in their decades-long conflict with Iraq. Meanwhile, Iraq received assistance from the U.S., the Soviets, West Germany, and others. When thousands of Kurds in Iraq were murdered with poison gas in 1988, the international community of states failed to act decisively, saying it was an internal matter of Iraq. But when Iraq invaded the *state* of Kuwait, the persecution of the Kurds was cited to justify war. Clearly, in the eyes of the world's states, Saddam Hussein's real crime was not that he was responsible for the murder of thousands, but that he crossed an internationally recognized state border.

One of the most urgent issues to emerge at the UNPO conference was the question of the options of peoples who are the victims of state violence. There was a passionate debate about armed rebellion and nonviolence. I was especially moved by the eloquence of representatives from the Baltic republics, who spoke of the strategies of nonviolent civilian-based defense that were so effective in their struggles. The conference participants eventually came to consensus on adopting the strategies of nonviolence. But we must develop and perfect nonviolent methods that are practical and effective: grassroots organizing, education, nonviolence training programs, lobbying the international community, establishing urgent councils, sending missions to areas of conflict.

For five hundred years, since the arrival of Christopher Columbus in the Americas, the Five Hundred Years' War of states against native peoples has continued. And with the collapse of communism in Eastern Europe, we see more and more ethnic conflict in the world. We must work to make the protection of human rights a touchstone of international politics. Questions of international law and human rights are indivisible; they are not internal state matters. We must listen to the cries of the oppressed and forgotten peoples of the world and challenge the claims of the state to absolute authority.

Most Americans I have met, even those deeply concerned about justice, think of Indian issues as a tragedy of the distant past. But the assaults against Native Indians continue in the U.S., Canada, and Latin America. While the Custer Period of direct military actions against Indians may be more or less over, at least in the United States, more subtle but equally devastating legalistic manipulations continue to block Indians from their land and their sovereignty. There are more than 1.5 million Indians in the United States. Many live in wilderness and desert regions, engaging in traditional subsistence practices on the lands of their ancestors. Many are independent nations, and they are not eager to become Americans, despite the economic, cultural, legal, and political pressures to do so.

A "nation" has a common culture and heritage, common language, stable geographic locale over time, internal laws of behavior that are accepted by members of the community, boundaries recognized by other nations, and formal agreements with other nations. By these or any standards, Indian "nations" are just that. The Western Shoshone Nation is one of many Indian nations still fighting the United States government. In the 1860s, the U.S. made a treaty with them recognizing their territory, which, according to international law, is still valid. Since 1946, the U.S. has attempted to extinguish many Indians' land rights by forcing financial compensation, but the Shoshones have always refused the money and thus still own their land. Still, large areas, including the Nevada Nuclear Test Site, were leased to the military and the Atomic Energy Commission, without consulting or informing the Shoshone. To connect the struggle against nuclear tests with the support of indigenous peoples' rights is an important task for the peace movement. In 1987, I sent a letter to the U.S. Congress stating:

> Recognized rights to land and common property are essential for the survival of a distinct indigenous people like the Shoshone. Their dispossession is an ethnocidal and genocidal act. The danger of nuclear tests is a global threat to all mankind and violates common human rights to health, well-being, and environment. We therefore demand you comply with the repeated appeals of the United Nations and stop nuclear tests immediately.... This protest is expressly directed at the violation of land rights of the Western Shoshone, the destruction of their land by militarization, and the damage of nuclear

fallout to the health of the people, the earth, and the atmosphere.

The native peoples' problem is directly related to the needs of wasteful technological societies to find and obtain remotely located resources to fuel our incessant demand for economic growth and technological fulfillment, and it continues because we in the First World want coal, oil, uranium, fish, gold, and more and more land.

Disregard for native peoples is made possible by the rationalization that our Western model of society represents the pinacle of evolution. Except for those in movements like bio-regionalism, deep ecology, and Green politics, most people in the West seem to agree about our so-called superiority. With this assumption, it becomes acceptable to humiliate and find insignificant any way of life or thinking that stands in the way of the kind of "progress" we have invented. (I have learned from my Tibetan friends how much more important spiritual progress is in comparison to any of the other forms of progress we have today. But we in the West understand so little about spiritual or moral progress.)

The American educational curriculum offers almost no information about Indians, making it difficult for young, non-Indian Americans to understand present-day Indian issues. Some European schools teach more about American Indians and Indian values than schools in the United States. One hundred percent "Americanism" has been pushed down the throats of people living in the United States, and many people now believe the U.S. is a homogenous culture, like Japan or Denmark, or at least it could be if it weren't for pesky minorities, immigrants, the alternative press, and other political troublemakers from the left. I have met students in the U.S. who were shocked to learn that every acre of what is now the U.S. was once part of some Indian nation. The Iroquois have been living in the northern U.S. for at least 5,000 years, and the Hopi have been living in the southwest for at least 10,000 years. (Some put it as high as 40,000 years.) By 1776, when the U.S. was established, only 100 Indian nations and two to five million Indian people, speaking more than 750 languages, had survived the slaughter of the fifteenth through seventeenth centuries, and were living in what was to become the continental United States.

Many also assume these aboriginal people had no form of government, but in fact, their forms of government were highly evolved and democratic. Systems of checks and balances, popular participation, direct representation, and a bicameral legislature were all part of the Great Binding Law of the Iroquois Confederacy, dating back to the 1400s. Between 1776 and the 1800s, through massacres and treaties, Indian land holdings were reduced by about 95 percent—from about 3 million to 200,000 square miles. Today, as the United States government and corporations seek to extract oil, copper, coal, and uranium from Indian land, they behave as they always have, but instead of relying on the cavalry, they now use legal manipulations.

Our assumption of superiority does not come by accident. It is soaked into the very fabric of Western religion, Western economic systems, and Western science and technology. Judeo-Christian religions are models of hierarchical structure. In this framework, all of these systems are missionary and colonial, embracing dominance. Our culture is using its machinery, as Jerry Mander states, to drive species into extinction by pure force.[4]

---

[4] Jerry Mander, *In the Absence of the Sacred* (San Francisco: Sierra Club, 1991).

If we want to reexamine our assumptions, we must begin by looking at certain unpleasant facts. Like many nation states, the United States was founded through violence and oppression. As an outpost for European colonialism, it was implicated in the conquest, decimation, and expropriation of the peoples who inhabited the continent, both Indians and Mexicans. After annexing half of Mexico's territory, the U.S. spent the next 150 years patrolling its borders in order to deport "illegal immigrants" from what was, in fact, occupied Mexico. If justice had its way, Mexicans would be granted special rights of immigration to *their* former territories. To assure necessary labor for the agricultural economy, the U.S. imported hundreds of thousands of Africans under a barbaric slave system that was to last two centuries. These were crimes of enormous proportion, and they set the nation on a path of racial division and conflict for generations to come. I am not pointing my finger in accusation. I am only attempting to look at the forgotten chapters in global history. Columbus Day for many is a day of mourning.

Environmental racism is another worldwide problem. Along the Mississippi River, between New Orleans and Baton Rouge, one-fourth of all U.S. petrochemical products are produced, mostly black people reside, and there is one of the most alarming cancer rates in the country. Most of the garbage incineration plants are near areas where black people live. Nuclear and toxic waste is stored on Indian reservations and in McFarland, California, where primarily Hispanic seasonal crop workers live, and many of the children are seriously ill from living on an old pesticide dump. Yet, environmental groups in the United States still have few minority members. In the Arctic homeland of the Inuit and the Dreaming Paths of the aborigines of Central Australia, military installations are now in place that continue to be key targets in the event of a regional or global nuclear war. In the industrialized countries, traditional indigenous lands are often misused for bases and military test sites, despite the cultural importance of these lands for the indigenous peoples. There are so many victims of nationhood. There are so many crimes associated with the founding of the United States. The repercussions are rampant in ghettos and on reservations.

And then there is the plight of children.We cannot remind ourselves too often that forty thousand children die every day and 15 million every year due to the lack of basic food and medicine. "The tragedy is not [merely] imminent," UNICEF Director-General James P. Grant said. "We are in the midst of it. And it will persist if the world does not finally decide to do something about it."[5]

In 1990, when the heads of more than 70 countries met to discuss the survival of children in the Third World, they allocated $2.5 billion per year to provide relief. That is the same amount of money spent by American companies every year on cigarette advertisements, by Soviet citizens every month on vodka, and by the world's militaries *every day* on armaments.[6] Shouldn't we give the children of the world a higher priority? Tens of thousands of young lives could be saved every year by the simplest means. Every day almost 8,000 children die of measles, whooping cough, and tetanus—fatalities that could be prevented by means of an inexpensive combined immunization. Every day almost 7,000 die of diarrhea, which dehydrates their

---

[5] *Der Spiegel,* 39/1990.
[6] UNICEF.

bodies; treatment with a sugar/salt solution would cost only a few cents. Every day over 6,000 die of pneumonia, which can be treated inexpensively. This silent death of vast numbers of children must and, I hope, will come to preoccupy politicians and compel them to seek to prevent it. UNICEF has calculated that in the 1990s, 100 million boys and girls will die if action is not taken. Susanne Mayer rightly states, "Anyone who wishes to talk about the life of children in the twentieth century must outline a scenario of death. Day in, day out, 40,000 children die worldwide. That makes 280,000 deaths per week and 15 million per year. These are obscene figures. They are evidence that vast numbers of children are dying. Some people call it genocide."[7] In view of the new, more open international political climate and disarmament in East-West relations, our governments must, at long last, present concrete plans of action to assist children. As UNICEF writes, "In the last decade of this century, this could be a unique present to the people of the coming century."

In the United States, 3 million children live below the poverty line. Children in the Western industrialized countries are dying from leukemia and cancer, for their environment has been shaped as if they did not exist. We need only think of Chernobyl, nuclear power accidents in Western Europe, and the chemical industry in Germany.

The situation of children in Asia, Latin America, and, above all, Africa is deteriorating drastically. Hunger, malnutrition, disease, homelessness, and slavery have been on the increase almost everywhere since the late 1980s. This is partly because of the heavy indebtedness of many developing countries. Time and again, the structural adjust-

---

[7] *Die Zeit.*

ment programs dictated by the International Monetary Fund require cuts to be made in social, health, and education expenditures. And as military and armaments budgets of inhuman regimes continue to rocket, their nations' meager funds are squandered on senseless armed conflicts. Germany's criminal exports of armaments and military installations must not be forgotten, nor must the Kurdish children who were murdered by poison gas as a result of German know-how.

The United Nations Convention on the Rights of the Child, which entered into force in September 1990, intended to help authorities take action against maltreatment of children. But one section of the Convention sanctions young people being called up for military service at the age of fifteen. In many parts of the world, minors are forced to fight in wars. The Khmer Rouge in Cambodia are notorious for their abuse of children in their "Killing Fields." And tens of thousands of children in South Africa boycott school in order to wage bloody wars in the townships. The children in the Israeli-occupied territories, and the children in Lebanon, Iraq, Northern Ireland, Tibet, Peru, Angola, and Guatemala are trained for active combat by the age of nine. In Guatemala, police have increased the use of force against street children. Dozens have been picked up, beaten, and tortured, and several children have died from the effects of torture. According to Amnesty International, Guatemala's National Police, which have for years received assistance with training and equipment from West Germany within the framework of a development aid program, is responsible for these murders.

Unfortunately, at meetings about children sponsored by the UN and others, young people play only a minor role. In future conferences, the children themselves should be given a chance to express their dreams and fears and to make proposals for improving the situation.

Children are dying because we let them die. It would be easy to save them. Amnesty International has rightly called upon all the governments of the world to take measures to protect children from murder, torture, and arbitrary imprisonment. In many countries, security forces do not shrink from making children the victims of repression. Every year, children find themselves caught between the military and armed opposition groups.

In developing countries one baby in twelve dies of malnutrition in the first year of its life. Ninety-seven percent of all infant deaths occur in Third World countries, where infant mortality is ten times higher than in Europe and North America. Moreover, life expectancy up to the fifth year is far lower than in the industrialized countries. And ever more children worldwide are developing malignant tumors. In West Germany the incidence of cancer in children rose by over 25 percent between 1961 and 1985. And during the 1980s, in the small town of Birkungen, Germany, one child in five was born with a deformity, evidently caused by a nearby dump. Children's rights must include the right to a healthy environment. The UN Convention on the Rights of the Child does not contain any provision expressly protecting children and their environment from avoidable effects of chemicals and radiation. The acute danger to children posed by noxious substances in the environment, which is increasing throughout the world, is ignored, underestimated, or considered taboo. The number of chemicals in existence worldwide increases by about one thousand every day. The amount of potentially noxious substances is further increased by the combined impact and interaction of chemicals in our foods, water, and the air we breathe. The ecological protection of children must become a subject that is widely discussed.

We can take action at local levels and give children a strong lobby. Anyone who makes plans for children should do so together with children, and, in my view, that means involving them in local decision-making processes. In local communities, children can participate directly in government. In other levels of government, we must find structures suited to children that enable them to participate in the political process. We must work to ensure that governments pay closer attention to the rights of children, enshrining their rights in constitutions worldwide. When will we succeed in protecting the most innocent people on our planet?

Human rights are for everyone. We must work to be sure that no one's rights are abused. Tomorrow it could be you, or me, who is tortured or imprisoned, or denied medicine, the right to travel freely, access to ancestral land, or the freedom to practice the religion we choose. We must work together.

Chapter Seven

German Reunification— A Missed Opportunity

"Our only hope will lie in the frail web of understanding of one person for the pain of another." —John Dos Passos

Most German Greens opposed the speed of German reunification. We had hoped for a confederation of two Germanys growing together slowly, with mutual respect, and for a nuclear-free, demilitarized, and socially just eastern Germany as a zone of peace in Europe. The Autumn 1989 East German Revolution was led in part by very strong women, among whom I count my dear friends Bärbel Bohley, Katja Havemann, and Ulrike Poppe, and by many other courageous women and men. I will never forget sitting in the tiny smoke-filled living rooms and kitchens of dissident friends in East Germany in the 1980s, where we discussed the power of the powerless, the power of ideas, and the power of the spirit, and shared dreams of a nonviolent revolution and a new society shaped by civic participation, even in the midst of great repression.

In December 1989, the Dalai Lama accepted our invitation to meet with the independent citizens and human rights movements, our dear friends whom we thought were going to become the new government of East Germany. On December 6—when Egon Krenz was still in power but about to resign—Gert Bastian and I accompanied the Dalai Lama into East Berlin. We were rather nervous, as I was risking my position by giving him access to an official vehicle. There was the possibility that the Dalai Lama could be arrested. But as we crossed Checkpoint Charlie, we knew that something was unusual. After years of being followed by the Stasi, East Germany's feared state security force, it was now the Stasi who were leading us in their little Trabis through the streets of East Berlin to the house where the legendary Round Table was about to begin. As we got out of the car, a circle of activists handed a candle to the Dalai Lama, who looked very beautiful standing there. Then, he placed a Tibetan prayer shawl outside of a Jewish old-age home, and we went to the Round Table.

There we witnessed the Citizens' Action Movement (CAM) adopt a very progressive constitution reflecting values of pacifism, ecology, social justice, and feminism, and we dared hope that the first revolution ever on German soil would bring about a new society with a greater degree of freedom and tolerance than had ever been known in Germany. The CAM promised the Dalai Lama that he would be the first official guest of their new state and that eastern Germany would recognize Tibet. We were all moved to tears by this momentous occasion. The Dalai Lama went on to Oslo to accept the Nobel Peace Prize and Egon Krenz resigned. But our dreams of a new East Germany were quickly reversed by Western politicians, bankers, and businessmen who, it turns out, were already lining up to invade the East with their old concepts and outdated economic and environmental solutions. Traveling between the two Germanys from December 1989 to March 1990, these West German officials brought with them their blueprint for "a perfect capitalist society."

Politicians on the right quickly reverted to nationalist rhetoric, and "being German" took on its worst, most arrogant meaning. In October and November 1989, East Germans had marched in the streets with signs and banners bearing the slogan, "We Are the People," meaning they were determining their own fate, goals, and future. But a few months later, West German flags began to appear on the scene, more and more German hymns were being sung, and suddenly the slogan was, "We Are One People." To me, this was the end of the revolution. In just a few short months, everything was turned upside down, and, in March 1990, in the first free elections in East Germany, the voters opted for a blueprint of West German society *à la Kohl* as a way to survive the post-revolutionary chaos.

West German Chancellor Helmut Kohl, NATO, the European Community, other Western countries, and even the Pope acted as if they themselves had personally liberated Eastern Europe and torn down the Berlin Wall. As Pastor Heinrich Albetz stated, "A West German military conquest of East Germany would have been more honest." Even Willy Brandt, from whom I least expected it, reverted to nationalist rhetoric, and in no time at all, nothing in East Germany was considered to be of any value, not even their universal childcare or liberal abortion laws. The only thing that seemed to matter was to "Go West," which ironically is the brand name of a German cigarette.

The East German people had little chance to consider the kind of society they wanted. Fear permeated all levels of society, and the citizens felt overwhelmed in the face of the Western invasion. They never had a chance to discuss the aims of their revolution or to determine the process of reunification. Our friends had dreamed of a better East Germany, not its dissolution. But by March, the media had all but forgotten the brave women and men who had been in the forefront of the revolution and the front lines of the October 1989 demonstrations, when Erich Honecker and his East German regime nearly opted for the Chinese Solution.

The dramatic reversal of the 1989 revolution was about money. In the Summer of 1990, armored cars transported 120 billion Deutsche Marks ($70 billion) to East Germany, and on July 1, millions of East Germans stood in lines at 10,000 bank branches and police stations to convert their Ostmarks into Deutsche Marks at the rate of 1:1, and then 1:1½ after 40,000 Ostmarks. In September, Chancellor Kohl had just one obstacle left—the disposition of Soviet troops in the East. He met with President Gorbachev and, in less than half an hour, committed $8 billion for the withdrawal and resettlement of the Soviet troops stationed in East Germany ($5 billion for 36,000 new apartments in the Soviet Union and the rest to pay for retraining the soldiers for civilian jobs) in exchange for a virtual guarantee that the treaty ending all postwar rights for the World War II victors would be concluded smoothly in Moscow. Considering the significance of the agreement, it is noteworthy that the signing ceremony took only five minutes.

On October 2 and 3, 1990, in Berlin's notorious Reichstag, we held our first joint session of Parliament, and the Unification Treaty was debated with surprisingly little passion. The Central Council of Jews in Germany had submitted a memorandum to Chancellor Kohl in July suggesting the following preamble:

> Aware of the continuity of German history and especially bearing in mind the unprecedented acts of violence committed between 1933 and 1945 as well as the resulting obligations towards all victims and responsibility for a democratic development in Germany committed to respect for human rights and to peace....

The German government submitted the following draft:

> Aware of the continuity of German history and bearing in mind the special responsibility arising from our past for a democratic development in Germany committed to respect for human rights and to peace....

During the debate, the Green Party stood alone in attempting to include the passage about the Holocaust in the preamble, and our efforts were unsuccessful. The government version received the majority vote, and it was not possible to include one word about "the unprecedented acts of violence committed between 1933 and 1945" in the Unification Treaty.

Chancellor Kohl then spoke about his hope for "a thousand years" of German happiness and prosperity. Imagine the insensitivity! That was the same phrase Hitler used when he spoke of "a thousand-year Reich." On October 3, 1990, Helmut Kohl signed a treaty giving West Germany full sovereignty in its merger with East Germany. In one fell swoop, nearly half a century of communism was abandoned, and East Germans came under West German rules on corporate and union practices, welfare, insurance, and other standards.

It was an eerie feeling when the East German government was formally dissolved. East German policemen and soldiers wore small plastic tags on their uniforms announcing that they were now West German. When asked how they could now serve under the West German government, they replied, "We are loyal to whoever gives our orders." Again we see the German who does not take responsibility for his actions.

Writer Günter Grass, one of the lone voices opposed to speedy reunification, spoke to the heart of the matter:

> Auschwitz speaks against even a right of self-determination, because one of the preconditions for the horror, besides other, older urges, was a strong, unified Germany. Not Prussia, not Bavaria, not even Austria alone could have developed and carried out the will and the method of organized genocide; it required a united Germany. We have every reason to be afraid of ourselves as a functioning entity.... We cannot get by Auschwitz. We shouldn't even try!

Since reunification, there have been increasing acts of anti-Semitism all over Germany, including the desecration of Jewish cemeteries, and a growing hatred of all who are *auslander* (foreigners)—not "German." The worst *has* come to pass. I have seen football hooligans singing songs about Hitler and winning the war against Jews and foreigners, neo-Nazis singing German hymns in the old text as they were sung in Hitler's time, foreigners being beaten in subway and railway stations. At one home for foreigners located near the end of a streetcar line in Magdeburg, right-wing groups came night after night, destroyed the windows and doors, and threatened the lives of the residents. In Ulm, right-wing extremists attacked a group of young Greeks, brutally beating a thirteen-year-old boy, and not a single German passerby stopped to help. Only when two Italian men and an Italian woman came to the boy's assistance did the skinheads leave him alone. The Ulm police commented, "No witnesses have come forward, so we have not been able to identify the offenders." What kind of state is this that fails to take adequate action to protect minorities against harassment and attack and allows foreigners to be intimidated, terrorized, and even killed?

In 1992 attacks on foreigners have been at the rate of more than one per day. More foreigners have been killed in attacks by neo-Nazis since the fall of the Berlin Wall than were killed trying to cross the border during all the years of communism. In the reunified Germany, Vietnamese workers and their families are experiencing more oppression and outright hatred than ever before. Intolerance and hatred have come out of the woodwork everywhere. It is not just the brutal acts of the neo-Nazis, right-wingers, and skinheads that are so alarming. What is even more frightening is that during these acts, in both West and East Germany, ordinary Germans have just passed by, looked on, or incited those committing the brutality. Klaus Hartung noted, "Their apathy, passiveness, and furtive delight do not feature in a single headline or TV picture. But this is the real threat. Everywhere people lack courage, and this is becoming a major domestic problem."[1] "Who would dare to chase and hit a skinhead?" is scrawled on a railway station in Berlin.

Neo-Nazi and fascist groups and skinheads have set Germany alight with hatred and loathing. The police in East Germany seem to be completely helpless against, if not actually sympathetic towards, neo-Nazis and skinheads. They often remain aloof when Nazi songs and chants are brawled, simply let people go on with organizing private militias, and usually arrive too late when there have been brutal attacks on refugee homes.

Teenage neo-Nazi groups did not count on so much unqualified support. Every night there are attacks on Ro-

---

[1] *Die Zeit.*

manian, Yugoslavian, Mozambiquan, and Vietnamese men, women, and children. As the neo-Nazis scream obscene slogans and pelt the foreign workers' hostels and homes with Molotov cocktails, stones, and bottles, groups of local residents look on and cheer, "Get the animals out." Foreign men, women, and children have tried barricading their streets with trash cans to ward off the attacks, but to no avail. In many refugee homes, there are not even telephones to call for help. My foreign friends in East Germany do not dare go out alone on the streets or travel by train late in the evening.

According to polls, 34 percent of Germans sympathize with the trend towards right-wing extremism. Ninety-six percent of those polled said they wanted fewer "economic refugees" in their country. At the present time, we in Germany, a country of 80 million people, have 5.3 million immigrants, and yet we cannot allow these people to live in peace.[2] Refugees and immigrants are viewed as nuisances who have crept in to sponge off of West German prosperity and throw the lives of Germans into confusion.

Many Germans feel threatened by foreigners who live, work, or seek asylum. Foreigners who have been living and working here for decades are still merely "guests," without voting rights even in local elections. Neo-Fascism and right-wing extremism are developing against this backdrop of xenophobia, revealing the historical link between fascism and racism. A fairly defenseless and isolated immigrant is particularly suited as a scapegoat for all unresolved tensions and problems. In Bavaria, as in many other areas of Germany, civic action groups have been set up to prevent the intake of more foreigners. Such blatant xenopho-

---

[2] *Der Spiegel.*

bia is rife with contempt for the weak, the foreign, and other social underdogs, and behind it lurks the threat of aggression and a willingness to use force. We can be sure that people from Vietnam, Mozambique, Cuba, Poland, Angola, or China were not included in the slogan of the revolution, "We Are the People." Heinrich Heine stated most aptly, "A German's patriotism means that his heart becomes narrower and contracts like leather left out in the cold, that he hates all things foreign and no longer seeks to be a cosmopolitan or a European, but merely a narrow-minded German." Herbert Leuninger added, "With its conduct towards refugees, the Federal Republic of Germany is gradually reaching the level of those countries from which people are fleeing to Germany."[3] There is a battle in our parliament and in the media about changing Germany's liberal asylum law. The Green Party remains fervently opposed to this.

There is also a debate in Germany about our willingness to abandon provincialism and be "normal" again, which means to play a larger military role on a global scale. Many of us fear that Germany's economic power will lead to military power, and a future militarist German nationalism with a nuclear capacity is something we must speak about realistically. Germany and Germans caused and were entwined in two terrible wars and attempted to eliminate the Jewish people from the face of the Earth. We must practice self-restraint, such as the ban on all arms exports, eliminating the military-industrial complex, no war financing, instituting a Peace Corps, and large-scale investment for ecological reconstruction in Eastern Europe and the South. Our German constitution guarantees antimilita-

---

[3] *Buntes Deutschland.*

rism, nonparticipation in global intervention, and giving political refugees asylum, but I am afraid we may alter all that for so-called normalcy. We must be watchful. All too quickly I heard Christian Democrats call for sending German troops to the Gulf as soon as the Constitution was changed. I heard it said that German soldiers would be superior to all others against Saddam Hussein. I heard suggestions that Germany should take a place on the Security Council of the United Nations and that we should have no qualms about becoming an economic and military world power.

The Germanization of the European continent—German economic imperialism—should not be underestimated. Germany as a whole will probably grow stronger, while the former East Germany will be kept as the "sick man." A German-led Europe, perhaps joined in time by Japan, will carry out the task of what Noam Chomsky calls "the Latin Americanization" of most of the former Soviet empire, with ex-communist bureaucrats running the branch offices of foreign corporations. Policies of self-restraint, demilitarization, and democratization—the most important signals Germany could give to the new and more powerful united Europe—are entirely absent. We should not underestimate the German government's influence in the European Political Union, as the Federal Republic is the largest financier, producer, consumer, and exporter in the European Community. Western Europe must become more modest and more in solidarity with those in the Third World, and must learn to share its incredible wealth with others.

The shameful history of the German weapons industry provides little assurance that we will be a responsible world power. Cases of weapons-export scandals fill the files of

German industry. Over one hundred German companies have been involved in sales of deadly arms to Iraq, Pakistan, South Africa, Iran, and many other countries, and arms exports remain one of the pillars of Germany's foreign policy. The U.S. sent more than one hundred formal notes of protest against planned German exports to a nuclear weapons factory in Pakistan, most of which apparently ended up in wastepaper baskets in the offices of the German ministries.[4]

A study by the U.S. Congress found that in 1989, Germany was the *only* country of the leading arms export nations to increase weapons sales to the Third World, from $830 million in 1988 to over $1.3 billion. The poisonous gas that Saddam Hussein used against the Kurds was made possible through German technology and the sale of German-designed plants for pesticide production. It did not bother them when Kurdish children were dying from poisonous gas, but our politicians worried that German soldiers might be killed by German-made weapons and chemicals. During the Gulf War, Germany donated and sold gas masks to Israelis and, at the same time, sold miniature gas chambers to Iraq so they could test the effects of the poisonous gas on dogs. And even the test dogs came from Germany. A new, united Germany cannot afford to act so arrogantly and immorally on the issue of uncovering export arms scandals. All too often Germans make a distinction between private and public morals. When the West German government promised to examine whether German companies assisted Iraq in building a poisonous gas factory, it took them nearly seven years to do this.

---

[4] *Nuclear Fuel*, March 6, 1989 (U.S.A.).

The "German question" was not invented abroad. It is a recurring legacy of our history. We have heard that "Nobody need fear the Germans," but, as Günter Grass put it, "We shall be united again, strong and clearly audible even when we try to speak quietly." The argument is constantly heard in the German Parliament that we should not hold present and future generations responsible for the crimes of the past. And so, the German government has never even passed a compensation bill for the forced laborers under the Nazi regime, thousands of whom are now dying in poverty. The Green Party and the Social Democrats have demanded that a fund for the compensation of forced laborers be created, but government advisors have never even investigated the matter.

There is also a movement in Germany to keep Russian Jews from immigrating. When the Green Party raised this issue in parliamentary debate, the government stated that it might be willing to let some Jews in, but how and when this will be done no one knows. For now, Russian Jews are not legally permitted to enter into Germany. I believe that every Jewish man, woman, and child who looks now to Germany for protection has the right to come here. We Germans have the responsibility to help in any way we can the Russian Jews coming who were able to survive the policies of the Final Solution. The arguments in Germany against Russian Jews have been shocking—that Germany is not an immigration country, that allowing Russian Jews in would create more anti-Semitism throughout Germany, that Israel would be affronted if Germany took in Russian Jews. We have a moral and historic responsibility to come to terms with our fascist past and also to come to terms with the East German communist past.

Although vast sums of money from the old East German ruling party went into the pockets of Erich Honecker and his cronies, there is still no provision for financial compensation for the victims of his regime. Even worse, after only three weeks of retraining, eight hundred former East German state lawyers and one thousand judges are now again in place in the German government. The personal files of thousands of bureaucrats were legally cleansed, making it difficult to trace the past careers of any of these judges or lawyers. It is all too reminiscent of what happened after Hitler's fall, when key persons involved with Nazi industry, jurisdiction, and security were treated with astonishing generosity.

A few leaders of the old communist regime are in prison or awaiting trial. Erich Honecker awaits trial in a military hospital near Potsdam, and a few others, like the former head of State Security, also lie in prison hospitals. But all the rest of Politburo and Co., who supported and were part of that same regime, are sitting in their villas pointing their fingers at Honecker. They lead their lives of luxury with illegally acquired wealth as if nothing ever happened and nothing has changed.

The Stasi files reported on the financial problems, sexual lives, and other personal details of 6 million people, including 2 million West Germans. Many East Germans understandably want to see their dossiers. They want to know if friends or neighbors betrayed them. Friendships are being tested as people ask themselves, Was I liked simply because I had access to spare parts? Was my neighbor an accomplice of the state security force, or does he suspect me of being one? Many are seeking psychiatric help to cope with such painful questions.

Between the two Germanys there is a strong psychological barrier—a Berlin Wall of the mind—a separation that may not be bridged for a generation or more. Many West German politicians speak of the two Germanys as if they are one, but they are not. The West thrived while the East lived under fifty-seven years of uninterrupted totalitarian dictatorship, from the Nazi regime to the Communist state. Many East Germans now see that their future is not established for them, and this is something they were not prepared for. Suddenly they have to cope with a whole new approach to life, and it is frightening for them. There is great uncertainty about property, rent, the reduction of social benefits, unemployment, and so forth. There is great distrust, as many fear they are being tricked or short-changed. Since the revolution of 1989, living conditions have undergone so dramatic a transformation that it is difficult to grasp the effect this has had on people. Those hit hardest by the skyrocketing unemployment are women, single mothers, the elderly, the disabled, and workers at the bottom of the hierarchy. Upper management, often made up of former party members, sit glued to their office chairs. One worker commented, "Some of those who claimed to be fighting for socialism under Honecker are now pressurizing us in a system of capitalism."

It will take years to repair the damage caused by four decades of Communism. The former East Germany will certainly change, but I hope that West Germany will also change in the process and become more modest and willing to learn. East Germany is bankrupt. Most of its eight thousand decrepit enterprises are on the verge of collapse, and the number of unemployed approaches 25 percent. The costs of building or upgrading plants and equipment, constructing roads, establishing communication networks, and cleaning up industrial pollution are expected to run to $455 billion, with estimates as high as $775 billion over the next ten years. And this rebuilding will not be done in an ecologically sound or decentralized way. It will be done in the hard capitalist way that is the norm in the West. Instead of developing soft energy systems, the West German nuclear power lobby is pushing its agenda, as if Chernobyl and Three Mile Island never occurred.

The East German school system is also in chaos. Many principals were fired because pro-Communist zeal was their sole talent, then half were rehired because of the lack of suitable replacements. German history of the last fifty years must now be rewritten and revalued for the third time. The Nazi-era work of Joseph Goebbels was followed twenty-five years later by that of his former pupil Margot Honecker, who, as Minister of Education, demanded that teachers implant hatred of capitalism in the hearts of East German children. The history they constructed must now be rewritten, the history books revised once again. One student summed up the confusion felt by many: "All this time we were told our country was the best and we achieved the most. Now they tell us it was all wrong." In a May 1990 meeting of East German authors in Berlin, Christa Wolf stated that she had the feeling that her life was being taken away. She explained that if you take away the identity that people have received for over forty years, you must replace it with something meaningful. You cannot just tell people that their lives and identity never meant anything at all.

In short, the process of reunification is proving disastrous. The legacies of the past, the damage of communism, and the exploitative opportunism of the West are leading to the collapse of social authority, the economy, and moral standards in the former East Germany. These conditions constitute a dangerous breeding ground for the types of populist ideologies espoused by the right-wing extremists. Mikhail Gorbachev was correct when he warned, "Nobody should ignore the negative potential that emerged in Germany's past."

The dangers posed by reunification are not confined to domestic issues; they extend to international policy as well. I worry about unified Germany's inability to handle its new power circumspectly and responsibly, both at home and abroad. I fear the Germanization of Eastern Europe through finance and loans, as well as other more subtle means of pressure and influence. A small possibility still exists to build new relationships in Europe that do not depend on the threat of military force. But there are still massive military infrastructures and huge stockpiles of weapons in place, and Chancellor Kohl has stated that membership in the European Community is only possible for those who want a strong military, economic, and political union developed along the lines established by the Western European nations. Given these signs, the possibility of a transformed Europe is small.

The influence of the independent citizens' movements has waned, as has their vision of a civil society. Jens Reich spoke for many when he stated, "We want to develop the political culture of the twenty-first century." The Round Table and the citizens' groups were forms of social self-organization intended to pave the way to a civil society and direct democracy. The German autumn of revolution called into question the representation of society exclusively by political parties, revealed values that transcend such parties, and achieved the direct exercise of influence by the public. But the West Germans gave the people of East Germany virtually no chance and no time to bring their own experience, ideas, and stimuli to mold the new state. The revolution ended all too quickly. We need a thorough public debate, radical democratic processes, and a new constitution as the foundation and expression of our efforts to jointly shape the present and future Germany. We must incorporate into the constitution more extensive ecological, democratic, and social rights, and renounce nuclear weapons and arms exports. A little self-restraint in the new German constitution would be for the benefit of all.

At the end of the second millennium, Germany has the chance to transform itself into a country of peace, human dignity, justice, and worldwide solidarity. Our hope for a peaceful and just Germany comes from the independent citizens' rights movements that led the revolution. Now we must all learn to become dissidents, so that together we can begin to build a civil society. There is so much we can learn from those days in the Autumn of 1989 about the possibilities of nonviolent transformation of society and the threats to it.

Chapter Eight

The New World Order

*"When elephants make war, the grass gets
trampled. When elephants make love,
the grass gets trampled. "* —African proverb [1]

As old empires fade and new states emerge, the world
is full of questions about whether or even when some of
the old demons will take control again. This is a time of
crisis and profound change. Belligerent nationalism and
demagogic populism are on the rise in Czechoslovakia.
Anti-Semitism is resurfacing in Hungary. Brutal, ethnic
warfare rages in the former Yugoslavia. In Germany, we
have seen the politics of discontent, intolerance, and fear.
After the hopeful, gentle, nonviolent revolutions of the
former Soviet bloc countries during the Fall and Winter
of 1989 that were all too brief, we are now witnessing all
of the old national and cultural identities reemerge, partly
with the positive desire for self-determination and democracy, but very much also as a revival of old hatreds and
fears.

As we Greens were celebrating the accelerating movements towards democracy, we realized that overcoming
the division of Europe in peoples' hearts and minds would
require *"détente* from below"—creating new forms of dialogue, Round Tables through which citizens could negotiate with governments and with each other. We had

---

[1] "Kikuyu Proverb," partly quoted in *Bartlett's Familiar Quotations,* 16th ed.
(Boston: Little, Brown, and Company, 1992), p. 784.

hoped for a nonviolent, democratic resolution of conflicts, and we applauded the Lithuanian government for making civilian-based defense the cornerstone of its security policy. We felt that a socially just, truly democratic, and demilitarized Europe could contribute significant solutions to the global problems and we wanted to expand the public, non-state, non-private sphere of activity, to create a truly civil space.

I was among the former Eastern European dissidents and Western European peace activists who met in Prague to found the Helsinki Citizens Assembly. We expressed our hope to create a new kind of security system and do away with military power blocs, to insure that it is no longer necessary to maintain troops on foreign territories, that all weapons of mass destruction be eliminated, and that military spending and conventional arms be drastically reduced. And we are making efforts to initiate a dialogue on future European cooperation, an extension of our "détente from below" strategy. We too want European unity, encompassing all of Eastern and Western Europe and the former Soviet Union, but we want this unity *in diversity*. We want a fully demilitarized and socially just Community—*not* a West European army and a West European Rapid Deployment Force intervening in future "resource wars," like the Gulf War, alongside the U.S. as a new European superpower. We want a multicultural Community that is open to the South, with full rights for all residents, refugees, migrants, and indigenous peoples, a Community that respects the rights of minorities and women, and respects ethnic, religious, and sexual differences. The present Europe does not look like this at all.

Right in the center of Europe, the tragic war in Yugoslavia has no end in sight, and no one seems especially concerned. In the 1980s, the deployment of nuclear missiles brought hundreds of thousands of people out onto the streets, but the brutal war in Yugoslavia brings out only a few nonviolent activists and Mothers for Peace. Where is the outrage? Cities are being bombed and populations strangled. Dozens of cease-fire agreements between Serbs and Croatians have fallen apart.

The sword of Damocles is hanging over Romania. In 1989, Romania alone underwent violent change, and it is steering again toward chaos due to left and right extremists. Alone in post-Communist Eastern Europe (except Albania), Romania has been denied Most Favored Nation status—a great irony considering that the U.S. granted Most Favored Nation to Ceausescu's regime, and for that matter to China. The effect of this has been that most Romanian products are excluded from the U.S. and EEC markets, thus discouraging international credits and investments.

In Czechoslovakia, there are scenarios for separate Czech and Slovak republics. Vaclav Havel was spit on by angry Slovak nationalists, and, a day later, pelted by eggs in Bratislava. He has tried desperately to keep the two halves together, and he wanted a quick move into European politics before it was too late. The game now is separatism through hatred, not building grassroots democracies through tolerance. Nationalist speakers play on ethnic passions. The impulse to split and be autonomous is understandable, due to the long suppression of ethnic groups. There are many historical reasons. But the impulse is not so much democratic as nationalistic and tribal.

The first free elections in Poland were a clear slap at reform—almost 60 percent of the electorate stayed at home. It did not take long for the euphoria of 1989 to give way to disillusionment. There is a fine line between the requisites of a market economy and the need to prevent social explosions. There will be 14 million people unemployed in Central and Eastern Europe, and over 25 to 30 million people unemployed in the former Soviet Union, the International Labor Organization predicts. In Poland, the former Communists finished in second place during the elections. In 1989, the Solidarity government took power with approval ratings of 90 percent. Now many Poles feel far worse off than before.

In the former Soviet Union, there are fears of massive hunger and energy crises. There is fear that the "Democrats" are ushering in the new authoritarianism on grounds that democracy cannot flourish amid economic and political chaos. "We cannot, especially during periods of economic change, be ideal democrats," said a Yeltsin advisor. He argues that pluralism and a free press hardly exist in the provinces, where old party bosses still rule. Is this the time for enlightened despots? The Soviet people are weary and alienated, and we have to be fearful about ethnic tensions and possible regional wars that could be fought with nuclear weapons *inside* the old Soviet Union.

Yes, the old demons are out again, not only in Eastern Europe, but also in Western Europe. In France, Jean-Marie Le Pen and his National Front Party have gained significant support. Le Pen campaigns against Arab immigration and Jewish influence. In a 1991 poll by *Le Monde*, 32 percent of the French people said they broadly agreed with his ideas. English philosopher Sir Isaiah Berlin has pointed out, "Nationalism is not resurgent. It never died, neither did racism. They are the most powerful movements in the world today."[2]

The parting of the Iron Curtain in Autumn 1989 revealed a land laid waste by industrial pollution. The environmental outrage of the people was so high that it helped topple governments in several countries. Now the task of ecological restoration is huge. Under the assault of air pollution and acid rain, many of Eastern Europe's medieval cities are blackened and crumbling, and entire hillsides are deforested. Crop yields are failing. Thousands of Bohemian schoolchildren wear breathing masks to walk to school. Rivers serve as open sewers, and clean drinking water is not easily available. One chemical plant in the former East Germany discharges as much mercury into nearby rivers in a single day as comparable plants in the West discharge in a year. To restore Eastern Europe's environment will be a massive undertaking. Estimates for cleaning up eastern Germany alone run as high as $300 billion.

The reasons for this environmental tragedy were the lack of public accountability, central planning, high government subsidies, and an orientation toward heavy industry. With the collapse of communism, Eastern Europe not only has a unique opportunity to correct these problems, but to surpass the West by implementing proven ecological strategies. As obsolete factories close down, they can be replaced by ecological and socially useful production facilities. But this is not happening.

Gert Bastian asked Czech Foreign Minister Jiri Dienstbier—for whom we had written many letters when he was imprisoned under the communists—why ecologi-

---

[2] *New Perspectives Quarterly,* Fall 1991.

cal and other alternative economic approaches were not being given a chance in the new, liberated Czechoslovakia. He said they lacked models because there were no Green think tanks and little environmental expertise. Many in the new government had been imprisoned for years and had missed the debate in Europe about alternative and holistic models of social transformation. And, of course, he spoke of the precarious economy and the need to give priority to protecting and creating jobs.

The shift to market-oriented economies took place with virtually no regard for the environment. Western businesses and governments made it clear that they are no more interested in ecological transformation in Eastern Europe than at home. They see only new markets where they can sell wastefully wrapped, asbestos-filled, PVC-coated, leaded products at an even greater speed. While faulty nuclear power plants are closing down in the West, the Western nuclear power industry is burgeoning in the East like a tragic boomerang.

One impediment to cleaning up the East is the huge debt load most countries there carry. With hard currency needed for debt repayment, few funds are available to invest in the environment. Poland and Hungary's debts, for example, are more than half their Gross National Products. Western countries could help by forgiving such debts in exchange for a commitment to spend the money on environmentally sound programs. One such offer by Germany could wipe $60 million in debt from Poland off the books.

One step to create a just and ecological economy would be to establish an ecology tax. Market economies have failed, for the most part, to take environmental costs into account. The cost of pollution created by industrial processes is generally borne by society as a whole, rather than by the consumer or producer of what was manufactured. To compensate for this and to create an incentive to minimize pollution production, Eastern European citizens' movements are asking their governments to adopt eco-taxes similar to those now under consideration by the Green parties in the West. There should also be efficiency standards, prohibitions on harmful materials, and other strong regulations. Government and business leaders must be made to understand that we are all united in one big mess. Environmental pollution spills across national borders. I still hope that an ecological model of economic development—an alternative to repressive state socialism and to aggressive capitalism—can emerge somewhere in Eastern Europe, perhaps in Poland, Hungary, or Czechoslovakia.

In the Winter of 1990, pollution levels in Czechoslovakia soared ten times past internationally accepted "safe" levels. The death of the Aral Sea, due to over-irrigation and chemicalization of agriculture in the Soviet Union, is another example of this destruction. But the sudden exposure of environmental problems in the East should not blind us to the many ecological problems resulting from the West's market economies. Aid and expertise coming from the industrialized North continue to be the main support for environmentally destructive development projects in the Third World. In this regard I can cite the large dam projects in India. The Third World will have to bear again the ecological costs of the North's new industrialism and consumerism, including the cost of cleaning up Eastern Europe. Eastern and Western Europe will increasingly use the Third World as a hazardous waste dump, and when transport to the Third World becomes too costly, the West will again turn to Eastern Europe as its dumping ground.

For Europe to become a true continent of peace, ecology, and nonviolence, we must begin to understand that 20 percent of the world's population has been using 80 percent of its resources, and that the planet is devastated. We must institute and practice policies of self-restraint. Our goal must be European unity in diversity through policies of nonalignment, active neutrality, and solidarity with the Third World. We must build a civil society, a fully demilitarized and socially just community, whose economic development will not be at the expense of the environment and the Third World.

We need to realize that it is our exploitative economics, industrial policies, and way of life, as well as our arms exports, development aid policies, and international finance lobbies—the World Bank, the G7, and the International Monetary Fund—who are responsible for the environmental degradation. We must not forget that it is our exploitation of Third World countries that has helped cause such grave poverty there. We cannot now simply turn away.

And we must not forget the dispossessed who are waiting at our doors. Today, a staggering 15 to 17 million people are refugees and maybe 30 million more are internally displaced. The opening of borders between countries of the European Community countries most likely means hauling up the drawbridge on the Third World people. We in Europe need to develop a sanctuary movement like that in the U.S. to assist and provide refuge for those who have escaped from war-torn and impoverished countries.World War II left 25 million people homeless. The dissolution of the Soviet Empire could cause an even larger dislocation, one unmatched in history. It seems that every nationality is rushing about in every direction in Eastern Europe—Hungarians fleeing Romania, Turks fleeing Bulgaria, the Roma and Sinti fleeing Slovakia and seeking jobs in the northern part of the country.

The peaceful transition of Europe is unthinkable without full observance and protection of human and civil rights. This is increasingly apparent as we witness the rise of racism in the former Eastern bloc. Discrimination against Africans and other Third World people is on the rise, not just in Germany but in all of Eastern Europe. And now, in their quest to return to "Europe," many in Eastern Europe are discarding the values of universalism and internationalism and promoting nationalistic chauvinism instead, as was demonstrated by the striking Ukrainian miners who demanded that all aid to the Third World be stopped. In 1988, 22,000 Africans were studying in the Soviet Union and Eastern Europe. In 1990, there were only 5,000.

The tearing down of the Berlin Wall, the collapse of the communist regimes in Eastern Europe, and the thawing of the Cold War brought the promise of a large-scale redirection of society's resources and priorities. We heard so much talk of peace dividends, from converting the permanent war economies, to ones geared towards addressing social and environmental problems. We dreamed about projects and programs that would be possible by redirecting some of the $8 billion a day from global military spending.

But our dreams did not last. There have been many changes, but few in the direction of restructuring for peace, ecology, or justice. Instead, we have seen the dashed hopes of the nonviolent revolutions of Eastern Europe, the ill-conceived and potentially disastrous reunification of Germany, and the brutal hypocrisy of George Bush's New World Order.

In the Summer of 1991, *Fortune* proclaimed that the world was beginning "A New American Century," echoing Henry Luce's essay of fifty years earlier, "The American Century," which demanded that the U.S. strive for world leadership. When President George Bush took up the theme and proclaimed a New World Order, I found myself distressed—it was not that many years ago that Hitler also called for a "New Order."

The post-Cold War era opened with the U.S. invasion of Panama to impose the rule of the 10 percent white minority, guarantee U.S. control over the canal, and send a message throughout Central America and the Caribbean: "We are the masters and you shine our shoes." The phrase "New World Order" surfaced in August 1990, when Iraq invaded Kuwait. The New World Order globalized the U.S. response to Iraqi aggression and included on its roster a veritable *Who's Who* of the world's tyrants, many comparable to Saddam Hussein. As Noam Chomsky wrote, "The United States and Europe will support the most murderous tyrant as long as he plays along, and will labor to overthrow Third World democrats if they depart from their service functions."

Bush enlisted Hafez Assad, the ruthless Syrian dictator whose troops still occupy part of Lebanon, into the alliance against Iraq. He campaigned vigorously to grant "Most Favored Nation" status to China, despite the Chinese leadership's barbaric treatment of Tibet and her own democracy movement. "We live," said Bush defensively, "in a world of lesser evils," a world in which there are few moral absolutes. Perhaps he was referring not only to

China but to his own of the killing of 300,000 people in East Timor when he was head of the CIA in the 1970s or support the U.S. and European governments' support of Pol Pot's regime in Cambodia. This New World Order does not look new. It looks like the same old *realpolitik*.

The Gulf War revealed that, in the absence of a Soviet counter-threat, the U.S. is now able to use more and more military force to expand its global influence and that it intends to do so. The West can no longer disguise itself behind the veil of defense against the Soviet Union, so Western governments, led by the U.S., are now looking to the Third World to find new adversaries. And the Gulf War heralded the dawn of a new era of high-tech warfare. The war turned Iraq into a bloody laboratory to test a new generation of weapons and hundreds of thousands of human beings perished there. Meera Nanda observed, "The 'smart bombs' pounding Iraq threaten to alter the international balance of power. They are meant to initiate a new *Pax Americana*—an absolute and unchallenged military supremacy of the United States all over the world."[3]

Third World communities and their environments always paid the highest price for the superpower rivalry. Between 1978 and 1988, weapons spending in the developing countries doubled, with the industrialized countries having established that armaments are an essential aspect of being an important member of the world community, while profiting from the sales of their arms exports. With the advent of the New World Order, the future looks no less grim for the Third World, as weapons producers and merchants are focusing even more on exports to Third World markets. Vandana Shiva writes, "With the end of

---

[3] *Third World Network Features.*

tensions between East and West, the Third World will increasingly become the supplier of raw materials for the new unified North and the dump for its hazardous wastes." I am certain that we will continue to see the subordination of Southern to Northern interests, with the industrialized countries—especially the U.S., Japan, and Germany—competing for who can most fully exploit their poor Southern neighbors. Worldwide branch offices of Western and Japanese corporations will certainly control the Third World by economic pressure or, if necessary, by governmental force.

The Gulf War was not just a war among nation-states, it was also a war against nature, a devastating blow to the ecology of the Persian Gulf. Beyond the ecological destruction that is always part of war, environmental terrorism was specifically used as an instrument of military strategy. By disgorging crude oil into the Gulf and torching oil wells, Saddam Hussein made the Earth one of his victims. The allied planes and missiles that pounded Iraqi nuclear and chemical weapons facilities (built with the help of Western companies) did the same. Desert Storm called to mind what we West German Greens said ten years earlier in our party platform:

> A lifestyle and method of production that rely on an endless supply of raw materials and use those raw materials lavishly also furnish the motive for the violent appropriation of raw materials from other countries. In contrast, a responsible use of raw materials as part of an ecologically sound lifestyle and economy reduces the risk that policies of violence will be pursued in our name. The pursuance of ecologically responsible policies within a society provides

the preconditions for a reduction in tensions and increases our ability to achieve peace in the world.

The world's militaries and arms industries are the greatest squanderers of desperately needed money, energy, raw materials, and human labor. Before leaving office in 1960, President Dwight Eisenhower warned of the dangers of the expanding military-industrial complex: "Every gun that is made, every warship launched, every rocket fired represents, in the final analysis, a theft from those who hunger and are not fed, who are cold and are not clothed."[4]

It is tragic that the extraordinary opportunities that came with the collapse of communism have been squandered. If there is any chance for us to learn from the nonviolent revolutions of November and December 1989, we must do so. There is no shortage of solutions to the problems we face. Many have already been tested on local and regional levels. The challenge is to develop the political will to do what needs to be done—to convert our war economies to Green economies. The Northern countries must come to understand that it is in our own interests to listen to the South, and not just force our outdated development models and economic structures on them in order to maintain our wasteful lifestyles. If we do not change our way of living and work for ecologically-based economic and political systems based on love and nonviolence, a New American Century under the authority of the New World Order will engulf us all.

---

[4] Dwight Eisenhower, "Farewell Address, January 17, 1961," quoted in Dean Albertson, ed., *Eisenhower as President*, (New York: Hill and Wang, 1963), pp. 162-163.

Chapter Nine

If There Is To Be a Future, It Will Be Green

"Many years from now, people will hear about the 1990s. A fragile era where a hydra of tensions and conflicts threatened the survival of the planet—terrorists menaced the innocent, racial and religious wars overtook great countries, and children became armed militia.... [But] the time was also marked by an uprising of the human spirit—people knew they could be trusted with Peace."—Carl Rogers [1]

The macabre scenario of Desert Storm proved many of the warnings and predictions we Greens have been expressing for so many years. In the almost prophetic peace manifesto published just after the Green Party was founded, we highlighted the devastating consequences of a consumer lifestyle and manufacturing methods that are based on the steady flow of natural resources recklessly squandered, leading to the violent appropriation of foreign raw materials. In this light, the Gulf War was a harbinger of future conflicts that will arise in the global struggle for increasingly scarce natural resources.

During our years in Parliament, we Greens persistently denounced the unscrupulous policy of arms exports to countries all over the world, in particular the criminal shipments of weapons' components to Iraq. The ministries responsible consistently reacted with bored arrogance, and our political demands for a halt to arms exports were voted down by the same people who later called for similar measures against Saddam Hussein. We also warned of the ecological catastrophes associated with militarism and of the

---

[1] Adapted from Carl Rogers, *Freedom to Learn in the 1980s.*

growing danger that environmental devastation could be used as a weapon in war. Even before the Iraqi troops set fire to the Kuwaiti oil wells, more than 1.5 million tons of crude oil had been poured into the Persian Gulf, more than sixty times the amount the Exxon Valdez spilled in Alaska.

The Greens have always taken the side of the victims of war, not only when Iraqis marched into Kuwait, but also during earlier and equally criminal acts of military intervention: China's rape of Tibet, Morocco's occupation of the Western Sahara, the Soviet invasion of Afghanistan, the Syrian war in Lebanon, and Israeli injustice towards Palestinians, to name a few. As a nonviolent political party, we have always supported the ethical principle that injustice cannot be repaid with injustice. We know that Sermon on the Mount civilism has to be inserted into politics and not saved just for Sundays at church. There is absolutely no justification for military violence. But our modest efforts to develop nonmilitary, nonviolent strategies for conflict settlement were met with weary smiles from the defense experts of all the established parties.

The failure of traditional military philosophy, with its hollow phrases like "just war" and "surgical strikes," was made tragically apparent by the Gulf War. The mass murder of innocent people did not solve any problems, but only created a host of new ones. Only an ecologically sensitive lifestyle and economic management based on the responsible utilization of resources can reduce the danger of crises like the Gulf War from occurring again and again.

So why did the voters turn away from our farsighted Green policies on December 2, 1990? On December 4, just two days after the elections in Germany, the *International*

Herald Tribune carried the headline: "German Greens: The Inside Outsiders are Back on the Fringe." The *Los Angeles Times* wrote: "The world's most prominent environmental party has become an endangered species after German voters lobbed the Greens out of the newly united nation's first Parliament." The defeat left many of us stunned.

But eight years of self-destructive and fruitless infighting among our various factions had paralyzed our political activities and created an atmosphere steeped in jealousy and distrust, and this was too much even for the Greenest voter. In the course of eight years in Parliament, our internal feuds grew worse and worse. We became intolerant, know-it-all, and smug about passing the 5 percent hurdle. In weekly intervals, we fought our battles in the most aggressive and inhumane ways, often denouncing each other, quarreling, and pointing fingers at whatever faction was unwelcome at that particular moment. We could not succeed if the ways we treated each other made more headlines than the substance and aims of our policies.

We came into Parliament in 1983 embracing a strategy of direct, nonviolent action outside of Parliament and effective, constructive participation within Parliament. We attempted to transform power from above into power from below to be used by all and for all. We hoped to convince everyone of the need for eco-justice in the context of ecological sustainability. Our first priority was to try to transform consumer mentality and our industrial economic growth system into an ecologically sustainable economy with conservation replacing consumption as the driving force, a basic ethic of restraint, a consciousness of limits that will enable people to act without degrading themselves or the environment. Ecology, social justice, nonviolence, feminism, antimilitarism, and anti-centralized structures were and are the main pillars of our program. Our clear and strong opposition in the early 1980s against the deployment of American and Soviet missiles, our clear and uncompromising stance on human and civil rights, and our radical answers to the grave environmental crises made it easy for us to enter the Parliament in 1983, where we offered a splash of irreverence to those somber chambers.

At the beginning of our parliamentary days, we had successes in many important campaigns, including civil disobedience actions on the Alexanderplatz in East Berlin, on Red Square in Moscow, in Turkey, in South Africa, and in many other areas of the world where human rights were not protected. We spoke out, daring to interfere in the affairs of other governments and even finding ways to cooperate across party lines on questions concerning ecology, human rights, women, and children's cancer. But as our successes grew, the internal power struggles among our factions became more and more aggressive. Some critics of the Green Party say that my conception and vision of the Green Party as an "anti-party party" failed, but I believe that it was not so much the radicalism of our agenda or program that failed or our desire to become a grassroots democratic party, but the way we practiced our political lifestyle with each other.

Some of my most painful times within the party were those concerning my commitments to human rights in Tibet and the democracy movement in China. Over and over, I was belittled and ridiculed by our dogmatic left-wing that seemed to become more and more selective on human rights issues. There were others who were not quite honest about why they had joined the Green Party, who saw nonviolence not as a philosophy and way of life, but simply as a tactic. Then there were those who preached civil disobedience, tax strikes, and sitting in front of military bases, but who never themselves participated. And there were others who voted with the idea to moderate the Green Party to such an extent that there would hardly be a need to negotiate in case of a coalition.

The 1990s were supposed to be our years, for we had been right about so many things, like Chernobyl, Exxon Valdez, and Bhopal. It was to be our decade, because the West German Greens had been the only party with continuous and close contacts with the independent citizen action groups in East Germany and the rest of Eastern Europe. Not one member of a major West German political party had been willing to write even a short letter during the 1980s to our independent citizen action friends in the East out of fear of upsetting the East German leaders. But, together with the citizen action groups of East Germany, we Greens developed visions for a nonaligned, demilitarized, and de-nuclearized Europe, including of course all of Eastern Europe. The Green Party remained an honest and necessary warning voice during the German reunification process, but our Green voice and Green agenda for the ecological transformation of East and West Germany were not heard.

Despite our defeat, our Green agenda for the ecological and nonviolent transformation of society has become a permanent fixture in German and European politics, and that is the case whether or not we survive as a party. We will survive as a party only if our electoral defeat is the starting point of a new learning phase for us. We have to confront our grievances and failings, beginning with structures, such as the principle of rotation, that have been upheld despite our experience that they make no political sense. I was pleased to hear Antje Vollmer, a longtime supporter of rotation, state in Bonn on December 4, 1990, "The incorporation of the rotation principle in the statutes of the Green Party was simply the expression of a pervasive climate of mistrust among the Greens which caused an unprecedented amount of distress to party members."

I am convinced that after the shock of December 2, 1990, the Greens in the regional and federal state associations will revert to the real Green priorities and principles—uncompromising nonviolence, radical ecology, indivisible human and civil rights, civilism, social emancipation, justice, and solidarity with the weak. This means freeing ourselves from dogmatism. I have never rejected the possibility of coalition with the Social Democrats outright, but future voting in Parliament on issues such as German participation in UN Peacekeeping Forces, deployment of troops in the Gulf, NATO, Turkey, halting the nuclear energy program, and the ban on arms exports will show whether the Social Democrats seriously intend to go ahead with renewal of their peace and ecology policies in the 1990s. As far as I am concerned, the most important and credible coalition partners of the Greens continue to be the committed human rights groups like Amnesty International and ecology groups like Greenpeace. These are the people whom we, the anti-party party, must be sure not to disappoint.

The term anti-party party has frequently been misunderstood. To me the term denotes a party capable of choosing between morality and power, that uses creative civil disobedience to combat every form of repression, that combines audacious imagination with efficient working methods, and that recognizes the link between world peace and peace within every individual. Anti-party parties do not exercise power in the old, authoritarian ways. They try to use power in ways that help people achieve self-determination in their own lives.

The Green Party in Germany has moved far away from this idea of an anti-party party, which was meant to be a movement like Greenpeace. We have become terribly bureaucratic, we have enormous interpersonal problems, and we have become very intolerant. I imagined we would be a party of internationalism and solidarity, but it is not the case. We are the richest Green party in the world, but all we do with our money is distribute it to our own voters and groups we associate with, instead of using more of it for international campaigns and solidarity. We have taken on all the bad features parties usually display—including financial scandals, a credibility crisis, and an inability to resolve problems in a constructive way.

We did manage to unite many different people and interests under one roof and survive this way for a long time. But as soon as we became influential and gained 8 or 10 percent at the polls, internal power struggles began. If we want to build up a movement to challenge the establishment, we cannot keep having arguments about who has the power of the party. All the different interests that comprise the Greens share the same goal, but we have big differences about how to get there. There is a strong oppositional trend, to which I belong—radical, feminist, and antimilitarist—and then there is the opposite trend that says we must come to an arrangement with the Social Democratic Party and make compromises. In between, there are many who want both—they say, if the SPD turns Green one day, then we can come together, but in the meantime we should keep our options open. So many divergent ideas about the way forward can destroy the party if each faction insists that only they are right. It would be sad if a "rainbow coalition" of diverse interests and viewpoints cannot work. If the West German Green Party breaks up, it will be difficult to build such a coalition again. If half the party says, "We can't stand it anymore, let's join the SPD," and the other half says, "We've had enough. We'll go back to our grassroots initiatives and little groups"—then the whole experiment of a radical parliamentary opposition in Germany will be finished.

But I would never say the Greens have no future. Internationally, we have a big future—in Austria, Ireland, Australia, New Zealand, and the Third World, for example. But I am not sure the German Green Party will survive. Sometimes, when I travel abroad, it is embarrassing how much faith people have in us. We get so much credit and people are so enthusiastic about our party that I feel I have to tell them some of these sobering things.

Another problem I see is that our program, which I still consider correct and necessary, was not really understood by our membership. Take the question of nonviolence. Nonviolence does not mean passivity or avoiding danger. It means not to harm anyone. When that is understood, we have a clear philosophy that helps us organize better and more activities. Many Greens say, "We are a nonviolent party," but if you ask them if they have been involved in civil disobedience, they have not. My colleagues in the parliamentary fraction often complained, "Oh God, Petra's got another court case!" They found it a nuisance that I still do these things.

Another substantial question that divides the Green Party is the question of the state. Some members say the

state is all bad. Others, like Otto Schily, have a more moderate view. I am in the middle. The state does many negative things, but it does guarantee rights. It is not enough
to say, "We have a good democracy." We must always develop and improve it.

We always speak of loyalty to the grassroots, but my
impression is that many of my colleagues do not really see
things this way anymore. We did not use the opportunities that being a parliamentary party gave us to help the
movement. We could have done a lot more with the information, connections, and funds we had access to as members of Parliament. We acted as if the Parliament and the
street were entirely separate. Greens in Parliament have
to act together with those outside.

I hope that other Green parties will learn from our
mistakes, especially our two-year rotation and other rigid
structures and pressures that punished those we elected
as speakers or leaders. Our party has not solved the problem of how to deal with committed, energetic, and credible personalities. Each time an individual stood out as
committed, working very hard for the party and receiving
much support, there was envy, jealousy, and constant attacks for the work that person did. Power in the old, traditional sense has become a very big problem for the Green
Party. There is more and more joining established power
at the top instead of transforming that established power
that we once rejected so clearly. A party needs leaders and
there will always be those who are prepared to put more
work into a movement than others. These people are not
necessarily above criticism. Honesty is required. The high
profile of leadership is a tool that must be handled care-
fully. But this does not mean doing away with leaders alto-
gether.

Despite all these problems, the need for Green parties is great, and I will continue to do my best to help Green parties flower everywhere. In the Summer of 1990 at a meeting in San Francisco, I urged the National Organization of Women to start a feminist, pacifist, ecological movement—a new political force, a U.S. Green Party or Green Forum or Green Alliance. I wholeheartedly support Jeremy Rifkin's call for a U.S. National Convention for a New Green Era. Of course, the process leading to a unified Green, feminist, pacifist, and ecological political platform will be frustrating and time-consuming, but you can learn a lot from our mistakes. You will have to confront the issues of careerism, rotation, mistrust of leading figures, grassroots democracy, and consensus. But we must do everything in our power to heal the wounds we have inflicted on our planet and on our souls. There is no other choice.

My Indian sister Vandana Shiva has stated, "There is only one path to survival and liberation for nature, women, and men, and that is the ecological path to harmony, sustainability, and diversity." If we all agree that the impact of science, technology, politics, and economics is inherently exploitative, there must be at last a real political, Green, feminist, pacifist, socially-just alternative. Green politics must put itself to the vote in the U.S. and become a political factor in all elections at all levels with credible, competent candidates.

Nearly a billion people on Earth live in dire poverty. Overconsumption threatens our planet. Massive debts are crippling the ability of Third World countries to provide even the most basic needs for their populations. Indigenous peoples and their environments are threatened. Two million dollars are spent each minute on the insane arms race, supposedly to keep the world safe. The consumer-oriented populations of the First World use grossly disproportionate amounts of the world's energy and resources, and burn most of the fossil fuels, thus contributing dramatically to the greenhouse effect.

There can be only one answer concerning when to start Green politics at every electoral level in the United States: *right now*. Because of the need for a low-energy future; because the Earth's remaining rainforests are being destroyed to meet the interest on debt repayments from poor to rich countries; because over 20 million Americans do not have enough to eat; because we must divert funds from military spending in order to solve terminal environmental, economic, and social problems; because human rights and civil liberties cannot be matters of political expediency; because we must replace consumption with conservation as society's driving force; because we can no longer ignore or neglect the years of warning signals telling us that we have come face to face with the natural limits of what we can take from the Earth; because the Earth has no emergency exit; because we can no longer sit by and watch Western governments be driven by endless expansion of consumption and by the futile goal of economic growth at any cost—for these and countless other desperate reasons, we must present Green alternatives in the U.S.A.

The Green political alternative in the U.S. must establish effective links between the everyday lives of people and the well-being of the planet. There is still a chance in the 1990s to consciously and democratically choose Green congressional and extra-congressional paths, the two complementing one another. Over the years, I have met many helpful and competent Green political groups and individuals in the U.S. who have inspired us in Europe to be more Green. There are many exciting and creative Green initiatives at the grassroots level here, and there is a desperate need to expose the long-term societal failures of the Republicans *and* the Democrats. For many years, American leaders have shown little understanding of ecology, pacifism, or social justice, not to mention feminism. I hope you will pour your hearts and souls into developing wise political alternatives.

As the British Greens stated, "Politicians up to now have fiddled with the planet and with our children's future and have brought us to the brink of disaster." A clear and credible Green political alternative in the U.S. is a road that can help many people. You can learn from our mistakes. The time for a U.S. National Convention for a New Green Era is now. The time for biosphere politics and life-affirming politics is now. If we learn to change ourselves, we can begin the difficult work of sharing our insights and way of doing things with others so that together we can do the work that is needed to stop destroying ourselves and to heal our Mother Earth.

Afterwords

The Legacy of Petra K. Kelly

MARK HERTSGAARD

More than anyone, Petra Kelly personified Green consciousness, one of the ascendant social forces of the late twentieth century. As a lifelong grassroots activist, and from 1983 to 1990 as a member of the German parliament, Kelly inspired millions with her rapid-fire indictments against the ecological dangers, social injustices, and spiritual poverty of modern military-industrial civilization. She was a leading figure in the European peace and human rights campaigns of the 1980s, mass movements that eventually resulted in the reversal of the superpower nuclear arms race and the collapse of Soviet totalitarianism. In recognition of her enduring historical significance, *The Sunday Times* of London in 1991 selected Kelly as one of the "One Thousand Makers of the 20th Century," placing her *vita* just before that of one of her heroes, John F. Kennedy. Impassioned, determined, self-sacrificing, Petra Kelly was a Mother Teresa with clenched fist—a nonviolent revolutionary striving tirelessly for a future where the meek really would inherit the earth.

Petra Kelly was born in Germany in 1947. When she was six, her parents divorced, her mother married John E. Kelly, an American Army officer stationed in Germany, and Petra took his last name. When she was twelve, the family moved to the United States, where she learned the fluent English that would help her become an international media figure. In 1966 she entered American University in Washington, D.C. Though she participated in the civil-rights and antiwar movements and also worked in the presidential campaigns of Bobby Kennedy and Hubert Humphrey, she was not so involved in the American student movement, according to Dr. Abdul Aziz Said, her mentor at American University and the man she later credited with teaching her about nonviolence. "She agreed with the objectives, but she felt that some of the student leadership and movement people were frivolous about it. They tried to *look* revolutionary but not really *be* revolutionary.... She was impatient that other students didn't care about hunger or human rights or other issues the way she did."

The ferocity of Kelly's passions was evident even then. Though she was still in college when cancer attacked her sister, Grace, somehow Petra managed to arrange an audience with the Pope for Grace and other members of their family. She later described the experience of watching Grace die as a turning point when she made "an emotional connection" to the dangers posed by radiation and atomic technology, and years after her sister's death she maintained a shrine to Grace in the back bedroom of her home in Tannenbusch.

After graduation, Kelly returned to Europe to write a dissertation and took a staff job with the European Community, but her real life's labor continued to be political activism. As a volunteer, she organized countless local citizens' initiatives in Germany, grassroots campaigns against nuclear power plants and airport expansions that were the precursors to the Green Party. Inspired by former German chancellor Willy Brandt, she joined the Social Democratic Party (SPD) during her twenties, but became disillusioned after Helmut Schmidt became chancellor in 1974. Schmidt supported nuclear power and the modernization of the NATO nuclear arsenal; Kelly saw him as a big step in the wrong direction. Indeed, the existing political parties of both left and right seemed hopelessly addicted to the status quo of economic growth at all costs, and blind to the ecological implications of living in the nuclear-chemical age.

A radical departure was needed. The Greens would be, in the words of Herbert Gruhl, an early Green leader, "neither left nor right—we are in front." The Greens would be different in another way as well. Borrowing from Eastern European dissidents, Kelly coined the term "anti-party party" to describe how the Greens would not be lured into the moral compromises accepted by traditional parties as the price of wielding power. Years later, she reflected on what she and her colleagues had attempted: "Albert Einstein once stated that the splitting of the atom has changed everything—except the way people think. And that is and was what we set out to do—to help change the way people think—to help people make their own grassroots decisions, to help them act locally and think globally." Recalling the famous slogan of the French students in 1968—"Be practical. Do the impossible."—Kelly added, "We, the generation that faces the next century, can add the more solemn injunction, 'If we don't do the impossible, we shall be faced with the unthinkable.'"

The Greens were a perfect vehicle for Kelly's radical, holistic politics, but it was not easy for such a romantic soul to leave the party of her youth. "Petra left the SPD in 1979, and she was always trying to persuade me to leave the Labour Party and join the Greens," said Mary Kaldor, one of the founding members of Britain's Campaign for Nuclear Disarmament. "But I remember her saying that when she left the SPD, she cried for three days at leaving the party of Rosa Luxemburg."

The Greens soon helped change the face of European politics by capitalizing on rising mass anxiety about nuclear weapons. The opportunity arose in 1979 when NATO decided to deploy Cruise and Pershing II missiles. The Cruises and Pershings were far more powerful and faster than their predecessors. They could reach their targets inside the Soviet bloc in a mere six minutes, a frightening whittling down of the nuclear hairtrigger. Meanwhile, in the wake of the Soviet invasion of Afghanistan, relations between Washington and Moscow had deteriorated to little more than the exchange of bellicose threats. The election of Ronald Reagan brought to the Pentagon officials who spoke of "winnable" nuclear wars. Reagan himself told reporters that, yes, he could imagine a "limited" nuclear war taking place in Europe.

All this stirred alarm on both sides of the Atlantic. By the Fall of 1981, the anti-deployment forces had grown strong enough to deliver a shocking blow to the political establishment. On October 10, some 250,000 people marched in a peace rally in Bonn. Similar demonstrations took place in London and other European capitals. Kelly's electrifying speech at the Bonn rally, a rally that made headlines around the globe, sealed her reputation as a media star. In the eyes of the outside world, Petra Kelly had become the Greens. Without the NATO missile deployment, the Greens might have remained an interesting, offbeat group on the fringe of German politics. Instead, they rode the deployment issue into Parliament. In the March 1983 elections, the Greens won 5.6 percent of the national vote and were awarded 27 of the Bundestag's 498 seats. Two of the Green seats went to Petra Kelly and Gert Bastian.

At the time he resigned from the army in 1980, Gert Bastian was one of Germany's most senior military commanders. He tendered his resignation in protest of the Cruise-and-Pershing decision, which he felt made accidental nuclear war more likely. As cofounder of Generals for Peace and Disarmament, a group of like-minded former NATO military commanders, Bastian helped author the so called Krefeld Appeal, a petition urging cancellation of the missile deployment that was eventually signed by five million people. For a man such as Bastian to resign, join the peace movement, and begin a romance with its leading spokesperson was unimaginable—roughly equivalent to Norman Schwarzkopf leaving his command and his wife and teaming up with Jane Fonda to protest the Persian Gulf War.

On the surface, Bastian and Kelly could hardly have been less alike. "She wore her emotions on her sleeve," said Sara Parkin, a founder of the British Greens and the author of *Green Parties*. "When she was happy, she laughed a lot. When she was sad, she cried. When she was angry, she stamped her foot. And he was not that way. He didn't show his emotions." Yet their devotion to each other was total. Charlene Spretnak, a Green activist in California and the coauthor of *Green Politics: The Global Promise*, remembered that when the two visited San Francisco in the mid-'80s, "Petra wouldn't even ride in a separate taxi from him." In her writings and speeches, Kelly often went out of her way to praise Bastian as her "close comrade and life's companion."

"I only met Gert Bastian with Petra a couple of times—a lunch and a dinner," recalled Abdul Aziz Said, "but one could see he was totally devoted to Petra and appreciative of her. One could see it in the way that he addressed her, looked at her, and spoke to her. One also saw that he saw himself as a pupil of hers, in a way. He looked up to her.... She was gentle toward him. They were definitely deeply connected."

Kelly's friends were constantly telling her to slow down, take some time off, be good to herself for a change, but it was no use. "Many times we would say to her, 'Petra, you are the symbol of ecology around the world, and what you are doing to your own body is anything but ecological,'" recalled Frieder Wolf, Kelly's legislative aide in the Bundestag. "She would smile and let you know that she knew it wasn't good for her health. But she was a revolutionary person who didn't think of herself, only others. Sometimes she would say, 'I don't know how long I will live, and I want to know I did as much as I could.'" "She was always talking as if on speed, and bouncing into meetings and saying, 'Let's do an action,'" said E.P. Thompson, the grand old man of the British peace movement, recalling how difficult it was to talk to Kelly about joint theory or strategy during their common struggle against the Cruises and Pershings.

Kelly's health had never been good. She had only one fully functioning kidney, and this chronic disorder gave her perpetually dark circles beneath the eyes. She frequently drove herself past all human bounds, and in 1982 she collapsed from exhaustion. Commenting on Kelly's manic schedule, a German magazine likened her to a candle burning at both ends. Her private response, recalled Erika Heinz, her best friend, was that "it is better to burn than to stop. The world isn't getting any better, so I can't stop." "Petra worked so hard, she couldn't have a normal life or a real home," recalled her friend Birgit Voigt. "Their home was more a library, an office. You could never find a place to sit down; stacks of mail and papers were everywhere, even in the kitchen."

Although Kelly wrote several books, the point of her speeches and writings, always, was to get people to act. "She used to lead one- and two-person demonstrations in front of the Bundestag, even when she was a member of the Bundestag herself!" recalled Monika Griefhahn, an old friend who later served as the environmental minister for the German state of Niedersachsen. Nonviolent civil disobedience was central to Kelly's worldview, and she and Bastian were arrested and fined repeatedly for their sit-ins at military installations. "She had a special approach to achieving political aims, one that was influenced by her American education," said Otto Schily, a German parliamentarian and former Green Party colleague. "She was outspoken, yes, but she also knew how to speak the language of symbols. When we went to the Kremlin together in 1984, we were ushered in to see Foreign Minister Andrei Gromyko. Once inside, Petra unbuttoned her jacket and underneath was a T-shirt saying, 'Arms into Ploughshares.' Gromyko was not amused."

Kelly regarded Mikhail Gorbachev as "one of the very few statesmen in the world who has understood…what the common environmental danger and the problem of human survival is all about." Yet this did not deter her from pressing the cause of Russian dissidents. Cora Weiss, a leading American peace and human-rights activist, was in Moscow in June 1988, when Kelly "asked me to join her in approaching Raisa Gorbachev at a reception for women.

Petra had a list of women political and religious prisoners then held in Russia's jails and wanted to know from the wife of the president why they were in prison and if she would work for their release. Mrs. Gorbachev's security detail struggled with Petra, stomping on her sandaled feet to try to get her away, but Petra refused to be intimidated and stood her ground. She always stood her ground." "The Greens completely confused the post-Stalinist Brezhnev types," said E.P. Thompson, "because here were people who were manifestly protesting Western policies, but also criticizing the Soviet policies."

Long before the Berlin Wall fell, Kelly and Bastian were among the first people to aid the fledgling democracy movement in East Germany. "Because they had diplomatic status, they were not searched when crossing borders," explained Erika Heinz. "So when they went to the East, their car was always full of typewriters, copy machines— all kinds of things. The dissidents there look at them as their greatest friends." "People who tell the story of 1989 underestimate the importance of the peace movement," added Mary Kaldor. "Of course the movement was critical regarding nuclear weapons because it changed the political climate and articulated proposals that Gorbachev could take up when he took office. But even more important was the involvement in what we called 'détente from below,' because it showed we weren't tools of the Kremlin. And as we got into it, the discussions with dissidents in Eastern Europe took on a life and importance of their own. You couldn't claim to be for peace and democracy and not take this issue seriously, yet a lot of people in the peace movement were quite fellow-travelers. Petra, on the other hand, was very consistent about her principles."

Gerd Poppe, a human-rights activist who later entered the German Parliament as a member of Bundnis 90, a Green Party affiliate from the former East Germany, recalled the solidarity Bastian and Kelly had shown him and his comrades during their lonely years under official repression. "Without the help of Petra and Gert and others like them, I would not sit in the Bundestag today," Poppe testified at their memorial service, his voice breaking. "The events of Autumn 1989 might not have come, or might have come much later. Or it might have been an autumn of blood, instead of an autumn of hope."

And so it was a special occasion when Kelly and Bastian traveled to Prague in February 1990 to celebrate Czechoslovakia's first free elections in more than forty years. No one personified the struggle for democracy in Eastern Europe better than Vaclav Havel, the playwright turned president. The trip was all the more special because they brought with them the Dalai Lama, Kelly's friend since 1984. Although raised a very strict Catholic, Kelly now embraced a mixture of feminist and liberation theology along with Buddhism, and was especially drawn to Buddhism's teachings about "not hurting anything, of being nonviolent, of finding God in yourself." It irritated her that Bonn officials were afraid to meet with the Dalai Lama for fear of offending the Chinese government, but there was no such reluctance on Havel's part; he made the Dalai Lama his first official guest as president. The visit lasted five days, five days of celebration, joy, and solidarity.

Yet even in the heady months after the Wall fell and nuclear arsenals were shrinking, Kelly found it hard to savor the epoch-making changes she had helped bring about. "She did not sit back and talk about how much good we had done," said her aide, Frieder Wolf. "She was always talking about what we had to do next. There were many moments when she clearly felt she'd accomplished something. But she was a person who was never satisfied. She always felt the misery of others. She knew that, however much she did, it was small compared to the actual reality of suffering in the world."

Pushing herself so relentlessly was not exactly a lifestyle of meditative Buddhist mindfulness, yet the Dalai Lama gave Kelly his blessing, according to Erika Heinz. "I doubt there was any human being on Earth who understood Petra better than the Dalai Lama," said Heinz. "He told her not to be quiet, to go on. And he said, 'I will meditate for you.'"

Milan Horacek, another of the Green Party founders, remarked with a smile that the Dalai Lama was the only person he could think of with whom Petra never had a controversy. "I knew Petra for sixteen years, so of course we had some huge fights in that time," Horacek continued. "She would yell and cry, bang a book on the table— whatever. I remember one time I had to grab her by the shoulders, force her out of the room, and lock the door against her. The next day she would come in with a little handmade present to make up. Petra had the whole palette of emotions, from very charming to very impossible."

"Petra was not a party person," said Christiane Gollwitzer, Kelly's dear friend. "She couldn't divide between love and politics. If she didn't like someone, she couldn't work with them." There were many in the Greens who didn't like Petra, or who at least distrusted her stardom. The Greens were determined to avoid personality cults and power trips, and this laudable goal was invoked against Kelly repeatedly. A year after joining the

Bundestag, she, along with Otto Schily, was forced to step down from her post as the party's parliamentary speaker. When the Greens developed the principle of rotation—requiring their parliamentary representatives to surrender their seats to another party member in midterm—Kelly refused to submit, arguing that rotation impaired efficiency and penalized competence. Nor was she willing to sit through the interminable discussions at party meetings, another sin against the party's egalitarian ethic.

"The German Greens assumed that Petra, who was clearly a charismatic figure, should also automatically be a great team player who was good at writing theoretical papers and all the other parts of building a movement," said Sara Parkin. "And that's part of their process of growing up. There should have been a job for her that let her be Petra Kelly, instead of expecting her to be like everyone else. I think a lot of her pain came because she believed in the idea of the Greens and tried to live the role they expected of her."

At the same time, there's no denying that Petra Kelly was a handful. Volatile, impossibly driven, a *prima donna*—those are characterizations employed by her *friends*. Throughout the 1980s, Kelly was embroiled in disputes with her colleagues. After she and her fellow Greens were obliged to leave Parliament following the December 1990 elections, when their party failed to poll the 5 percent national electoral support needed to stay in power, the estrangement deepened.

When Kelly lost her seat in the Bundestag, after seven-and-a-half years in office, she suddenly found herself deprived of the tools of her trade. Gone was the infrastructure—the telephone, fax, and photocopier—she had relied on to cultivate her worldwide network of activist contacts. Gone, too, were the platform and legitimacy conferred by her status as a member of the German parliament. No longer could she embarrass human-rights abusers with resolutions like the one she introduced in the Bundestag in 1987 condemning China's policies in Tibet. No longer could she threaten corporate polluters with official penalties if they failed to clean up their act. And, worst of all for someone whose forte was promoting radical ideas among the general public, no longer could she take access to the news media for granted.

Kelly remained a figure of interest, especially to the foreign press, but the fact that she was now a mere private activist made journalists in Germany and elsewhere regard her as inherently less newsworthy. "She was very down about this— she would complain to us about it," recalled Erika Heinz. She briefly hosted a television interview show in Germany, but her advocate temperament did not suit her role as program moderator, and the arrangement came to an end amid mutual recriminations in March of 1991.

To be sure, none of these setbacks led Kelly to retreat from her political commitments or relax her grueling schedule. The suffering in Tibet was a priority issue for her in this period, but she remained active in a host of other causes as well, including working for the enlightened treatment of child cancer victims, an enduring passion since the death of her sister. She continued to receive hundreds of letters a week from around the world; doggedly, she insisted on answering each one herself, routinely staying up until four and five in the morning to write her replies in longhand.

Petra Kelly and Gert Bastian died in October 1992. According to the official police description, Bastian shot Kelly in the temple while she slept in their suburban Bonn townhouse, then walked outside their bedroom and shot himself in the top of his forehead. There were no signs of struggle or burglary. The bodies had lain undiscovered for at least two weeks.

Some among Kelly's global family of friends and comrades refused to accept the official version of events, contending instead that she and Bastian were victims of politically motivated assassins. However, among Kelly's closest personal friends, virtually none believed in a third-party conspiracy. The conspiracy scenario was contradicted most powerfully by the powder burns found on Bastian's hands. True, it is conceivable that these could have been faked, but only by killers representing an extremely sophisticated and powerful organization, such as the former East German state police. Ten years previously, in the early 1980s, when Kelly was leading the charge to overturn the nuclear arms policies of the superpowers, such a scenario would have made tragic sense. The political eclipse she had undergone in recent years, however, made it much harder to credit the idea that it was her activism that had provoked fatal retaliation.

The full truth of Petra Kelly's death may never be known. The available evidence suggests overwhelmingly that it was indeed Bastian who shot Kelly, but Peter Matthiessen is absolutely right that "something was missing, something was not known" about their deaths. Important questions remain, gaping up from the rainy ground of history like an empty grave. The police, for example, left open the question of whether Kelly was shot with her foreknowledge. Thus the moral stain of suicide, with its unbecoming overtones of weakness, surrender, and political despair, hangs over Petra Kelly's legacy, almost certainly wrongly. This is an injustice that her erstwhile colleagues in the German Green Party might try to correct by seeking an independent inquiry into the killings, but as of early 1994 they have refrained from doing so.

An independent investigation, with access to all relevant records held by the German government, including the former East German authorities, should have been undertaken, and still should be. Government prosecutors did affirm in their final report that nothing in these records sheds additional light on the deaths of Kelly and Bastian; however, there has been no independent examination of these records. The laws of Germany allow the government to withhold the records from the public and the press, so in the absence of sufficient political pressure, the matter is, unfortunately, likely to rest there.

Whatever the exact cause of her death, the legacy Petra Kelly leaves behind is breathtaking. In the words of Frieder Wolf, "There is only one person in a generation like Petra." If a human race still exists two hundred years from now, Petra Kelly will be remembered somewhat the way we remember Joan of Arc today, except that Petra Kelly led a movement that fought not merely for the life of a single people but for all life on the planet. American President George Bush boasted in 1992 that he had ended the Cold War and vanquished the nuclear threat. If any individual can make so grand a claim, Petra Kelly has a greater right to it.

Her role in reversing the suicidal superpower nuclear-arms race and in spreading democracy within the former Soviet bloc will loom largest in her legacy. But the injection of ecological concerns into corporate and governmental decision making throughout the world and especially in her German homeland also deserves mention. Though she herself was never satisfied, the fact is that Germany became the world's most environmentally conscious industrial nation, thanks largely to the efforts of the Greens. "So many things they were pushing eight years ago have become mainstream issues," observed Lester Brown of the Worldwatch Institute. "For example, their positions on nuclear power, recycling, demilitarization. Germany has begun to condition its foreign assistance on a Third World country keeping military spending within reasonable levels, making it the only country I know of to do that."

"Maybe it is my Eastern soul, but there are things in life we don't understand, and for me Petra's death is one of them," remarked Professor Abdul Aziz Said, Kelly's college mentor. But Said did offer a metaphor, the metaphor of root and branch: "The roots of the tree become buried, but the continuity of the tree is revealed in the branches. It is true the physical body of Petra has been buried. But we still can see her presence in her absence, in the branches of her life—her concerns, her connectedness to those in need, her commitments. And new branches will continue to grow."

A Living Memorial

CHARLENE SPRETNAK

Delivered on December 14, 1992, in San Francisco at the
Memorial Service hosted by the California Green Party.

Petra Kelly was one of the most remarkable members of
the postwar generation, someone who determined at age
thirteen that she would become either a nun in a Third
World country or a new kind of politician. When she died,
in October 1992 at age 44, international news agencies
called her "perhaps the world's best known environmen-
talist" and "the personification of the German environmental and peace movements." She was not only the most
widely known Green in the world, but the person through
whom a transAtlantic synergy was brought full-circle.
German Greens had been influenced in the sixties and
seventies by observing the ecology, peace, feminist, and
social justice movements in the United States. Petra then
brought to America during the eighties charismatic testi-
mony about the combination of those concerns in the new
phenomenon called "Green politics."

Petra was uniquely positioned to play such a role, having spent her childhood in Bavaria and her adolescence
in the United States, after her parents had divorced and
her mother had married a U.S. Army colonel. While earn-
ing a degree from American University's School of International Service, Petra worked in Robert Kennedy's
campaign and Hubert Humphrey's office and was influenced by the nonviolent civil disobedience of the civil

rights and antiwar movements. Returning to Europe, she worked as a policy analyst for the European Economic Community and then cofounded the West German Green Party in 1979. She was elected to the West German parliament in 1983, along with twenty-six other Greens, and remained in office until 1990.

Petra Kelly expressed the Green perspective to the international press with passionate concern and commonsense logic. Her performance on "Meet the Press" in 1983 was so impressive that a conservative, hawkish journalist who had grilled her during the program told her afterward that he wished she were on the other side.

Throughout her political life, Petra refused to regard politics as a cynical game of tactical maneuvering, power plays, and undercutting one's opponents. Instead, her method was simply to decry the violations of the human spirit and the entire Earth community that she saw, whether they were located in the ideology of the nuclearized nation-state, in various government policies, or in Machiavellian behavior. She maintained a spiritual sense of goodness and grace at the heart of life and never accepted a jaded view of the human condition. That is why she was literally astounded, thousands of times over, to learn of unfairness, duplicity, and cruelty. She felt that exposing such violations with righteous indignation and substantive documentation would surely mobilize opposition and make possible a healing correction.

In the early years of the West German Green Party, Petra was central in forging the links between peace issues, environmental concerns, and feminism. She coined the term "anti-party party" to express her sense of the new political mission: serving the grassroots movements *and* operating internally in ways that actually embody nonviolence on all levels. That second principle has proven to be the more radical one, demanding a highly self-aware rejection of the competitive dominance modes of interaction that inform Western socialization. Instead, the West German Green Party played macho "hardball politics" internally and replicated many of the worst dynamics that had preceded them in alternative politics. Two fiery, warring factions, neither committed to the full meaning of nonviolence, dragged the party down into a self-destructive paralysis.

For Greens and other activists worldwide who are trying to develop political processes that avoid the toxicity so apparent in contemporary politics, the fact that the bodies of Petra and her companion, Gert Bastian, were not discovered in their Bonn apartment for nearly three weeks is a painful reminder of the extent to which she had been marginalized by her German colleagues and isolated in her last years. Like many other Greens, she had been pushed out of the party by dynamics of *realpolitik*. In Petra's case, resentment toward her media attention was a factor, though she had spread the Green message extremely well. Petra and Gert continued to work on behalf of eco-social causes, speaking out in their final years against the Chinese occupation of Tibet and also the rise of neo-Nazism in Germany. Petra was also drawn to eco-feminism and its support for the struggles of grassroots women.

In Petra Kelly the concern for eco-social justice in our generation seemed distilled to a unique intensity. It poured forth from her in myriad ways that will continue to engender new political possibilities.

How might we memorialize Petra in our own activism? I believe that the radically Green principles and ideals she stood for will live on in the eco-social movements around the world. The aspect of her political legacy that does need attention and nurturing, and could benefit our movements immensely, is her focus on verbal nonviolence, an ethics of care, and sensitivity to the way people are treated in politics. The Green project will surely fail if we cannot live out the vision in our own circles. That has been the message of countless activist women, but it is still considered peripheral by far too many people.

My proposal for a living memorial is that we remember the tragic passing of Petra Kelly and the fact that she was deserted even in death for three weeks—and then think about any sincere activists or former activists in our movements, Green parties, organizations, and institutes who may have felt unappreciated, or unwelcome, or pushed aside. Seek them out and apologize on behalf of all of us. Ask them to give us another chance. Invite them back. Embody the vision.

For Women Who Dare

In the weeks following Petra's death, a tension developed between those of her peers (mostly activists outside of Germany) who felt that the unanswered questions at the scene of the shooting certainly indicated the need for a thorough investigation and those of her peers (mostly in the German Green Party) who staunchly opposed any suggestion of such a need. To this day I do not understand the resistance.

During those intial weeks, the media noted that the German Greens were "strangely silent" about the deaths of Petra and Gert. This seemed to me a reasonable reaction, since they had treated her so badly over the years that a good deal of soul-searching was in order. Far from expressing appreciation for her tireless work as a cofounder of the party and her brilliant expositions of the Green vision to the German and international press, they had assigned watchdog committees to hound her, had done a great deal to marginalize her, and—after she and all the other Green parliamentarians lost their seats in the Bundestag in the 1990 election—had refused to give her a job or a grant from their foundation in order that she might have office support to continue her Green and human rights work via her extensive networks in both the industrialized countries and the Third World.

Speaking at her memorial service in Bonn on October 31, 1992, which was hosted by the Green Party, a man who had long been prominent in German Greens issued a rare acknowledgement that the party had not treated Petra well and had not understood what they had in her. It was a long-overdue *mea culpa* but certainly an understated one. A *mea maxima culpa* would have been more appropriate, considering that the speaker—an ambitious pol who had led one of the warring factions during the 1980s and subsequently maneuvered himself into the leadership of the party, and is thought by many to be headed for national office—had relentlessly denigrated Petra over the years, even at the height of her political success, with the standard left-Green put-down of being "politically naive" (read: from an activist background other that Marxist or anarchist).

In late 1992 I heard from various sources that a widespread attitude about Petra's death among politically engaged Germans (not necessarily members of the Green Party) was the following: "Who cares how Petra Kelly died? She had outlived her usefulness. She was neurotic. She was so dependent on Gert that she would have been put into an institution long ago if it hadn't been for him." A German acquaintance explained this to me as an unremarkable response in a "callous culture."

I was stunned. So—they absolutely would not forgive this woman her world-class success as an inspiring activist and her international media presence during the heyday of the German Green Party some eight or nine years earlier. Neurotic? She was an intense, intelligent, fast-talking woman who managed to function effectively under enormously stressful conditions—and to persevere. I would be hard-presssed to count all the famous male politicians in history who were "neurotic" in their dependence on a spouse or lover to ease their exhaustion, soothe their exasperation, and heal their psychological wounds. That entire side of the male political career *is not even mentioned* in their biographies. It most certainly is not cited as a justification for heaping scorn upon the deceased activist or politician and dismissing the worth of his life's work.

Petra in death demonstrated one last feminist insight, a painfully acquired realization: much less is accepted, overlooked, and forgiven in women who dare to have a public presence than in their male counterparts. The benefit of a doubt is not extended. Her missteps and shortcomings are perceived in exaggerated proportions. Her commitment and admirable traits count for little. She is not supported. She often fights in isolation. A collective sigh of relief may be discerned when she is contained, thwarted, or discarded and resigns "for personal reasons." She is supposed to have known better than to trespass into a forbidden realm.

But you didn't, Petra. All you knew—and wanted to know—was that the needless suffering of children and adults, of forests and rivers, of the entire Earth community could be stopped if you and countless others would speak out and dedicate yourselves to creating new possibilities. Your concentrated efforts on behalf of dozens of just causes were informed by a luminous orientation I can only call "pure heart"—although you would probably say you were energized by the Gandhian power of *satyagraha* (truth force) and nonviolence.

I have heard now that women around the world—and probably some men as well—cried and cried when you were killed. I did.

You were so loved, and you'll not be forgotten.

A Personal Tribute

ELEANOR MULLONEY LECAIN

When I first met Petra Kelly, she was rushing into a press conference in the German Bundestag, like a colt on the run. It was 1982, the Greens were in Parliament, and Petra was becoming well known as a spokesperson for new ways of thinking and being. She was briefing the press about her upcoming trip to the United States where she would address the Council on Foreign Relations, talk shows, and of course grassroots peace and environmental groups.

We hit it off instantly, like old friends. She had an engaging smile, when she wasn't talking. She spoke in a rapid-fire manner, as if speaking were a channel for her enormous energy. Her eyes sparkled, full of life and love and fight.

We corresponded for the next ten years. Corresponding with Petra often meant getting an appeal to help on a crusade, like fighting for human rights in Tibet, usually with a personal note about her latest adventures. Petra felt deeply the suffering of the world. It was as if her heart were connected to all people, and to the Earth. If anyone were injured, she felt injured. She was not the kind of person Mark Twain wrote about when he said, "I love humanity, it's people I can't stand." Petra loved humanity *and* people *and* the planet. Even with her hectic schedule, she found time to send me a telegram and gift on my wedding day.

In 1984 Petra came back and spoke to the San Francisco Women's Party for Survival, which I had helped organize. Her visit coincided with a visit by Geraldine Ferraro who had just been nominated as Vice President on the Democratic ticket, the first woman to reach that position in a major party. Her nomination was a lightning bolt charge for those of us interested in women in politics. When I brought her to hear Ferraro speak, Petra turned to me and said, "*She* should be the Presidential candidate!" Petra passionately believed that women's voices must be heard, and that we women must own our own power, if the planet is to survive.

I took Petra and her companion, general-turned-pacifist Gert Bastian, on a tour of San Francisco Bay. As we passed Alcatraz Island, I told her it used to be a prison holding such characters as Machine Gun Kelly. "Machine Gun Kelly!" she exclaimed. "That's what they call me because I talk so fast!" At the time I thought she talked fast because she had so much to say; years later, I wondered if she knew she didn't have much time.

Petra looked exhausted, and several of us encouraged her to relax for a day or two. Much to our delight, she agreed to go to Yosemite National Park for the weekend. For two days, we walked through the hills and valleys of Yosemite. She couldn't remember the last time she took two days to relax; she told me she usually slept only five hours a night.

"Where do you get your strength?" I asked her.

"My sister," she said, without batting an eye. "She died of cancer at a very young age, and I swore I would do everything I could to prevent suffering like that. I do not want her to die in vain."

The last time I saw Petra was in November 1991, at the World Women's Congress for a Healthy Planet that Bella Abzug organized. We arranged to have dinner after her meeting, which meant we started eating about 11 pm. Petra told me about the book she was planning to publish, the book you now hold in your hands. We had dinner the next night also, just Petra, Gert and me. She told me about the dream she had of opening a human rights office in Bonn, and about the internal struggles of the German Greens. We talked about U.S. politics, and what might be done here. She told me tales of her latest adventures, like meeting Richard Gere ("I didn't know who he was!" she exclaimed), and being in Jane Fonda's house as she introduced friends to her fiancé, Ted Turner.

The last time I heard from Gert was in September of 1992 when he called me to ask my support for Petra getting the Sakharov Human Rights Award. In the course of a long phone conversation, Gert expressed concern about Petra's health, and particularly about the German attacks on foreigners. "There are attacks daily!", he said. "It reminds me of the days of my youth, when Hitler was on the rise."

A few weeks later, I learned that Petra and Gert were dead. I was shocked. No! She's too young! Not now! Not this way, by a gun! She who lived her life for peace and nonviolence, ripped from us violently, like a female Gandhi. I find it hard to believe Gert would kill Petra given his devotion to her. Besides, he called me on her behalf just about a week before they died. We may never know the circumstances of their deaths.

We can only speculate what she might have accomplished had she lived another ten, twenty, or thirty years. But we can appreciate what she achieved in her forty-four years.

Petra Kelly was a driving force in the German Green Party which put forward a strong program for peace and ecology and which helped spark the dramatic rise in environmental consciousness in the 1980s around the globe.

Petra had an incisive mind and an open heart. She understood why things are the way they are—who benefits from the status quo, why they resist change, and how change happens. She understood how most people, especially women, feel powerless, and that the way to get through that was to take action. And she believed passionately in nonviolent transformation to a more peaceful, just, and ecological world.

The scope of Petra's impact could be seen at her memorial service. Hundreds of messages came from all over the world, from Chinese students, Kurdish people, Israelis, Japanese, Bengalis, Irish, and of course Tibetans.

Petra Kelly was a woman with the courage to speak her truth, and the determination to bring about needed change. She inspired me and countless others with her clarity of thought and her courage. She published numerous articles and books on ecology, feminism, peace and human rights including this, her last.

Thinking Green! is a real tribute to Petra and a great service to the planet. It is our last chance to hear from one of the most brilliant and courageous women of our century. As I read *Thinking Green!* I hear Petra's voice, loud and clear, warning us of the dangers of current directions and pointing the way to a more ecological, peaceful future. She lays out her vision one last time, in the most powerful and compelling way ever. If you are moved by what Petra says, then decide what action you will take in your own life for the principles she espouses. As you act, know that Petra is with you, for wherever people stand up for human rights, women, peace, or ecology, there Petra lives.

Contributors

Mark Hertsgaard is an international investigative reporter. He is the author of *On Bended Knee: The Press and the Reagan Presidency* and *Nuclear Inc.: The Men and Money Behind Nuclear Energy*. He travelled to Germany in October 1992 to investigate the death of Petra Kelly for *Vanity Fair* magazine.

Eleanor Mulloney LeCain speaks and writes on creating a more humane and ecological future. She is active in politics for women, ecology, peace, and sustainable jobs, and has served as Massachusetts Assistant Secretary of State for Strategic Planning, Executive Director of Blueprint 2000, and founding Council member of The Elmwood Institute.

Charlene Spretnak is active in Green party politics. She is author of *The Spiritual Dimension of Green Politics, States of Grace, Lost Goddesses of Early Greece*, coauthor of *Green Politics*, and editor of *The Politics of Women's Spirituality*.

Resources

Many peace, environmental, human rights, and women's organizations are doing the kinds of work Petra Kelly worked so hard for all her life. This sampling of groups in the U.S. was compiled by Eleanor LeCain and Allan Hunt Badiner.

Amnesty International
322 Eighth Avenue
New York, NY 10001
(212) 867-8878, fax (212) 627-1451

California Green Party
P.O. Box 3727
Oakland, CA 94609

Center for Defense Information
1500 Massachusetts Avenue NW
Washington, DC 20005
(202) 862-0700, fax (202) 862-0708

Community Media Project
1415 Third Street, Promenade Suite 301
Santa Monica, CA 90401
(310) 458-4588, fax (310) 317-4911

Consortium of Peace, Research, Education, and Development
c/o Insitute of Conflict Analysis and Resolution
George Mason University
Fairfax, VA 22030
(703) 273-4485

Council on Economic Priorities
30 Irving Place
New York, NY 10003
(212) 420-1133, fax (212) 420-0988

Cultural Survival
215 First Street
Cambridge, MA 02142
(617) 621-3818, fax (617) 621-3814

Earth Island Institute
300 Broadway, Suite 28
San Francisco, CA 94133
(415) 788-3666, fax (415) 788-7324

EcoNet/Institute for Global Communications
18 De Boom
San Francisco, CA 94107
(415) 442-0220, fax (415) 546-1794

Elmwood Institute
P.O. Box 5765
Berkeley, CA 94705
(510) 845-4595, fax 845-1439

Environmental Defense Fund
257 Park Avenue South
New York, NY 10010
(212) 505-2100, fax (212) 505-2375

Friends of the Earth
1025 Vermont Avenue NW, third floor
Washington, DC 20005
(202) 783-7400, fax (202) 783-0444

Greenpeace
1436 U Street NW
Washington, DC 20009
(202) 462-1177, fax (202) 462-4507

Greens/Green Party USA
P.O. Box 30208
Kansas City, MO 64112

Human Rights Watch
485 Fifth Avenue
New York, NY 10017
(212) 972-8400, fax (212) 972-0905

Institute for Asian Democracy
1518 K Street NW, Suite 410
Washington, DC 20005
(202) 737-4101, fax (202) 347-6825

International Campaign for Tibet
1518 K Street NW, Suite 410
Washington, DC 20005
(202) 628-4123, fax (202) 347-6825

International Human Rights Law Group
1601 Connecticut Avenue NW, Suite 700
Washington, DC 20009
(202) 232-8500, fax (202) 232-6731

Lawyers' Committee for Human Rights
330 Seventh Avenue, 10th floor
New York, NY 10001
(212) 629-6170, fax (212) 967-0916

Natural Resources Defense Council
40 West 20th Street
New York, NY 10011
(212) 727-2700, fax (212) 727-1773

Peace Action
1819 H Street NW, Suite 640
Washington, DC 20006
(202) 862-9740, fax (202) 862-9762

Plutonium Free Future International Women's Network
2018 Shattuck Avenue, Box 140
Berkeley, CA 94704
(510) 540-7645, fax (510) 540-6159

Political Ecology Group
571 Valley Street
San Francisco, CA 94133

Positive Futures
815A Viejo Rostro
Santa Fe, NM 87505
(505) 984-0641, fax (505) 820-6722

Rainforest Action Network
450 Sansome Street, Suite 700
San Francisco, CA 94111
(415) 398-4404, fax (415) 398-2732

Refugees International
21 Dupont Circle
Washington, DC 20036
(202) 828-0110, fax (202) 828-0819

Unrepresented Peoples and Nations Organization
100 West 92nd Street, Suite 29G
New York, NY 10025
(212) 799-4822

Women's Action for New Directions
691 Massachusetts Avenue
Arlington, MA 02174
(617) 643-6740, fax (617) 643-6744

Women's Environment and Development Organization
845 Third Avenue, 15th floor
New York, NY 10022
(212) 759-7982, fax (212) 759-8647

Worldwatch Institute
1776 Massachusetts Avenue NW
Washington, DC 20036
(202) 452-1999, fax (202) 296-7365

Parallax Press publishes books and tapes on mindful awareness and social responsibility. Some recent books include:

Learning True Love: How I Learned and Practiced Social Change in Vietnam, by Sister Chân Không

Love in Action: Writings on Nonviolent Social Change, by Thich Nhat Hanh

Dharma Gaia: A Harvest of Essays in Buddhism and Ecology, edited by Allan Hunt Badiner

Seeds of Peace: A Buddhist Vision for Renewing Society, by Sulak Sivaraksa

Touching Peace: Practicing the Art of Mindful Living, by Thich Nhat Hanh

World as Lover, World as Self, by Joanna Macy

The Anguish of Tibet, edited by Petra K. Kelly *et. al.*

For a copy of our free catalog, please write to:
Parallax Press
P.O. Box 7355
Berkeley, CA 94707